GH00865396

A

Story to Be Told

Copyright © 2011 Sally-Ann Taylor

Cover design by Brent Atkinson THIRTY5IVE.com

All rights reserved. No part if this book may be reproduced by any mechanical, phonographic or electronic process, or in the form of phonographic recording; nor may not be stored in a retrieval system. Transmitted, or otherwise be copied for public or private use – other than "fair use" as brief quotations embodied in articles and reviews without prior written permission of the publisher.

ISBN 978-14477-21475

"As I scattered the ashes in the sea,
A single yellow rose came back
On the crest of the wave"

A Story to Be Told
The synchronistic events of a Psychic Medium

By

Sally-Ann Taylor

This book tells the true story of the events in her life. All of the stories told are taken from genuine readings. Some names have been changed to protect the identity of the clients and people in the book.

For Angel

For teaching me to be the person I
have become.

For Yesterday, Today
And All of Your Tomorrows

Taylor :0) xx

There are so many people to say Thank you to.

Thank you to my children and family for understanding my special job.

My friends and you all know who you are,
for being with me on my journey and supporting me.

A special thank you to my friend Karen Rowley, for giving me the encouragement and the daily chats to keep me focused and help me to understand.

For Kay and Ken for your inspiration, wisdom and support on my pathway.
Nicky, without you I would never have written this!

A special thanks for the special men in my life.

Brent who is the most fantastic friend and amazing graphic designer and for designing my posters and the book cover!

Malcolm for his wonderful support and keeping me sane!

Paul for his inspiration and wisdom and for never doubting me!

Not forgetting the most amazing clients who have trusted me to work with their loved ones and sharing in their lives.

Without you all, my life would be without meaning.

The Early Years

My story begins on the 31st March 1960 the day on which I was born. It was however much later in life that I realised how synchronistic this date was, but before I continue with my story I would like to give you the significance of my birthday.

On the 11th December 1847, the Fox family moved into their house in Hydesville, New York. Several tenants had vacated the premises due to mysterious noises. The family started to experience problems until March1848. Moving furniture, noises and raps were heard at night.

This increased until 31st March 1847 when there was a very loud noise and continued outbreak of unexplainable sounds. The house was searched thoroughly but no explanation for these happenings could be found.

The youngest daughter, Kate realised that the sounds were in response to the noises made by the family. She started to ask for answers by the snapping of her fingers, thus being their first communication with the spirit world. This contact was established by getting it to rap once for yes and twice if the answer was no.

Mrs. Fox herself tested the noise by asking it to rap her children's ages. It did so correctly, including a child that had died in infancy. She then asked if the noise was human, no answer was given, but when she asked if it was a deceased person she got a strong knock.

By continuing to ask yes and no questions she was able to find out that the spirit was gentleman aged 31 he was a peddler that was murdered for his money and goods which were in the house. He was buried in the cellar. Further questions revealed the spirit was also willing to communicate with the neighbours who also had correct answers given to their own questions.

Digging in the cellar started on 1st April to see if anything could be found. Unfortunately water poured into the hole and attempts were abandoned until the summer months. They dug down five feet where they found a wooden plank, deeper below this was charcoal and quicklime. Finally human hair and bones were discovered, they had come from a skeleton which was confirmed by medical experts.

Another 56 years elapsed before the rest of the skeleton was discovered. Parts of a rough wall had fallen down which was a yard away from the original wall of the cellar. There was a peddler's box found with the skeleton.

The manifestations continued most nights until it became too disturbing. The family had to leave and take up residence with their married son David. The raps continued and one night over 300 people conversed with the invisible spirit.

Even though they left the house Mrs. Fox was convinced the spirit had followed her daughters, so the girls were split up. Kate went to live with her brother in Auburn and Margaret stayed in Rochester with her other sister.

Unfortunately these plans didn't work because other manifestations and raps broke out in both places. The ones in Rochester were very violent. The disturbances continued until a visiting friend Isaac Post remembered that Leigh's brother had used the alphabet to converse with the Hydesville spirit.

In answer to the first question, the following message was spelled out. "Dear Friends, you must proclaim this truth to the world. This is the dawning of a new era; you must try not to conceal it any longer. When you do your duty, God will protect you and good spirits will watch over you". After this message was given there were many communications where objects moved, tables rocked and guitars were heard playing, psychic touches were also experienced.

On November 14th 1849, the first public demonstration was given in Rochester at the Corinthian Hall. A committee was instructed to validate the Mediums and the spirit world phenomena were experienced. Two more committees were selected and they both validated that the Mediums were indeed genuine.

Professional Mediumship began on the 28th November 1849 owing to increased sitting by Leah. As the movement began to grow, Kate Fox trained other Mediums in her circle.

The movement has gone from strength to strength from these original experiences; fortunately Mediumship has progressed from the yes and no answers that were given many years previously.

So you can now understand the significance of my arrival into the world half a century ago and my future as a Psychic Medium. Obviously at the time I was born, my parents Carole and Tom Fowler had no idea that their daughter would one day be writing a book about her rather strange work.

I love my Mum and Dad very much, but I have to be honest and say neither one of them are believers of this work. Maybe one day they will understand about it and how bringing their daughter into the world has affected so many people.

I cannot remember much about my early childhood, but I do remember the day my brother Tom was born. I was shunted off in a neighbour's car to my Grandmother, in those days childbirth at home was the normal thing. I remember waiting in anticipation to find out if I had got the Sister I wanted, but I was happy to have a little brother.

As a child I used to spend a lot of time on my own, I never really got on very well at school and the other children avoided me. I couldn't really understand why, but perhaps they sensed I was different to them. I used to spend a lot of my time in the garden talking to the birds and bees and any animal that would listen. I wasn't aware that I had any psychic ability but I understand now that I was picking up a lot from the animal world that I spoke to and they did talk back, but when I used to mention it, people were horrified. I also had lots of imaginary friends, which I now know were spirit children. When I spoke about such things I was told that if I was not careful I would end up in a mental hospital. I learned very quickly from an early age not to speak of such things.

My school life was really horrible; I hated it and was forever suffering from sore throats. I wasn't a very good pupil and had many blackboard rubbers thrown at me because I was daydreaming. But I always went to school on a Tuesday and Thursday as these were the days I would walk down and see my Grandmother for lunch and tea!

After school one day I was making my way to my Grandmothers for tea. My journey used to take me down a hill and at the bottom was a bus stop. As I started to walk down the hill I saw a man waiting for the bus and he absolutely terrified me. I don't know why but I was unable to walk past him. I started to cry and walked back up the hill. One of the boys from school was coming down and asked me why I was so upset. I told him that I was really frightened but I had no idea why. He said he would walk down the hill with me so that I felt safe. After we went past the bus stop, I turned to go up the lane leaving my friend to go home and I ran all the way to my Grandmother's.

I realised later in life that this was probably my first experience of picking up on people's Auras. We all have an energy field around us which is called an Aura. Some people see colours around bodies, but usually it is just a white light. Every living thing has an Aura, if you take your eyes slightly out of focus and look at plants and trees, you will see the energy field around them. You may have to practise this a bit, but it is fascinating when you start to see them.

In the holidays and every Sunday I used to go and visit my Gran and Grandad. My Grandad for some unknown reason was the kind of person that people didn't take to. He had lots of near misses when he was in the Navy and he told me many stories of how he left ships and they sank and also how he was knocked into the sea by an anchor which left a huge scar all down the middle of his body. By rights he should have left the earth plane years before he did. He had so many accidents and strange things used to happen to him.

He wasn't my birth Grandad, my Gran had remarried, but we were very close and I used to spend a lot of time with him on his allotment. He used to teach me all about the plants and herbs and the things you could make from them. Nothing got wasted on Grandad's garden. Even the potato peelings were used to make potato wine! Grandad used to make a lot of wine and there were bottles everywhere, it used to drive my Gran nuts. But I was partial to his carrot wine and I have never tasted anything like it since. I know it was probably wrong at my early age, but I was always given a little tipple. That said I guess it stopped me from going out and trying alcohol as a teenager and getting carried away with it, like a lot of them do.

I think it was Grandad that inspired my love of gardening; I always liked to be close to Mother Nature. Gardening is a love that I have carried all through my life. My Gran on the other hand, inspired my love of cooking. I used to love going for Sunday lunch, Gran would always spoil me and she used to cook rock cakes, and coconut tartlets which hardly had a chance to cool before I demolished them. When we went shopping she always taught me to buy the best meat I could afford, food was so important to the diet and a hearty meal would give us the sustenance we needed.

One of the days that stand out in my life was the 8th April 1969. I remember it as though it were yesterday. I had just turned 9 years old and I was standing in the playground. The weather was unusually hot and I was standing on my own against the wall. One of the dinner ladies came out and started to tell the teacher that a girl had gone missing. Her name was April Fabb and she was 13 years old.

April had gone for a bike ride to visit her sister and brother-in-law when she had disappeared without a trace. The thoughts that went through my head were of panic and despair as I wondered what had happened to her.

The stories continued for months after, police were called to search her area of Metton, but sadly April was never found. As you read further into the book, you will understand the significance of this story of the missing schoolgirl.

Shortly after this had happened, the family moved into a new home. As a very small child I was filled with despair at the thought of leaving the familiar school and friends behind. My new home was much nicer and it was near to fields, much different from the city home I had spent years growing up in.

My Dad worked day and night to save up the money to buy the house outright. He didn't believe in having any debt but wanted to give his family a better lifestyle. I always remember him telling me about the hours he had to work making wrought iron gates and mending cars to raise the £3,000 he needed. It was a lot of money in those days. If only houses were still that cheap.

My first day at the new school was very daunting. We lived quite a distance from it and I had to walk miles to get there. Dad would always take me in the mornings, but we were always late. I really hated being late as it drew attention to me, which made me feel really sad. Quite often I would be so worked up by the time I got there that I would be sent home again because I looked so ill. Even to this day I hate being late for anything and usually end up being too early instead.

Just before I went into high school, a new addition arrived in the family. Now I had two brothers to contend with. There was much discussion as to what to call the new arrival. We all had our favorite names, so eventually they were all put into a hat and my brother became known as John Kevin David!

High school was a nightmare and I absolutely hated it. I never felt that I fitted in and it became more and more obvious that I was different to my peers. I had made friends with two other girls but I was very much the wallflower. I struggled every day with my lessons and had really strange feeling about people. Obviously I was picking up on their energy fields.

One day I was sitting in a maths lesson, I was terrible at maths, and a girl turned round to me and started goading me. She was a very pretty girl and very popular with lots of friends around her. As often happens there are always groups of people that cling together. I was a plain Jane and definitely not part of the in crowd.

She kept saying things to me and wanting me to tell her how brilliant she was. She kept saying that she wasn't very good, in the end I agreed with her, not knowing what else to do.

Her reaction was to slap my face really hard. I was horrified and embarrassed and ran from the classroom.

As I was very much a loner, I thought I would have problems with her group of friends. I dreaded the next break time. To my surprise this event caused a real stir as news was passed through the different years about what had happened. I was prepared for the other students to either ignore or have a go at me but to my surprise the reverse happened. Everyone started to turn against her; she was so used to being popular that she hated having the situation reversed.

I on the other hand was enjoying being popular. The situation was getting out of hand and I could see her really struggling, I began to feel sorry for her and finally accepted her apology. In the end I had chosen to learn my first spiritual lesson of forgiveness, thus my popularity grew and I started to be more accepted by the in crowd.

Looking back on what happened from my perspective as a spiritual person, I understand that as I was learning what it was like to be an outcast, I still had to forgive her. Her lesson was about vanity; she was always telling everyone how beautiful she was and asking people what she looked like. The thing is appearances can be deceptive and even though she was beautiful on the outside, she certainly wasn't on the inside.

I kind of think she learned her lesson because I saw her twenty years later working in the local supermarket; She had plans of being a beautician whilst she was at school. But she was one of the first girls to get pregnant at fifteen and didn't make it to college. The pretty girl at school had turned into a very sad looking and overweight person. I had to look twice at her as I didn't recognise her until she spoke. Life had not been very kind to her she told me as she put my shopping through the scanner. Clearly this showed in her face, she had aged a lot more than me and really hadn't looked after herself. I felt sorry for her and said that I hoped her life improved.

This experience left me with a compassion for other people and to this day I will always stick up for those less fortunate than myself and I always give the time of day to people that appear to be struggling on their own.

Life at school still continued to be difficult, although I was more accepted, I still spent a lot of my time on my own. My best friend, Sandra was as guilty at missing school as me, so we quite often missed each other. But we did enjoy each other's company. We used to go into the city on a Saturday and meet. We eventually got Saturday job's working together at the local Woolworths.

I had started to feel very unwell, more so than usual. I had been suffering with pains in my side for months. I spent so much time at the doctor's but they never seemed to get it sorted. I was eventually given medication to take for the pain. I had felt really unwell all day and started to walk home. As I was walking along I suddenly lost my eyesight. I was so frightened and I didn't know what to do.

A lady saw me struggling and crying, I had wandered onto the road, she offered to walk me home and I was really grateful. When we arrived at my house my Mum phoned the doctors immediately. She was told that I needed to stop the medication, apparently the tablets I had been given were normally used for violent convicts in court to subdue them.

The blindness lasted for several days and it taught me what it was like to experience the different senses of touch, smell and hearing. Nothing happens without a reason and I do feel that I was being prepared for being more reliant on my other senses, which I now use a lot more in my work. It also made me realise how reliant we are on other people. When we lose one of our five senses, it makes the others work more efficiently.

I know that this particular experience opened me up more spiritually. My psychic awareness became more fine-tuned, the trouble was I didn't realise what it was or why it was happening. I found that I was more sensitive to the people around me, picking up on their emotions and reactions. I started to become aware of when things would happen, I knew if people were going to call round or if they were going to feel unwell. What a shame I didn't understand more, it would have stopped me getting into all sorts of trouble.

In 1974 I was to receive my first warning from the spirit world, but I did not understand what it was all about. On the Sunday afternoon I received a phone call from a friend called Maxine, asking if I would meet her at the local shop. I didn't want to go, but she told me that Harry wanted to meet me. Harry was my first love and I would take every opportunity to sneak out and meet him. My Dad was very strict and boys were a definite no, so I agreed to meet her.

As I walked down to the shops, I began to shake from head to toe. I couldn't understand why I was feeling this way. As I approached the row of shops, I saw my friend waiting, but there was no sign of Harry.

Suddenly I was grabbed from behind and I felt hands around my throat, someone started to pound my eyes with their fists. I eventually fell to the floor. My nose was bleeding and I was badly cut and bruised. My attacker ran away with my so called friend.

I hobbled home and my parents were shocked at the state of me. My eyes were so swollen from the attack that I couldn't see. The police were called and they came to take a statement and arranged for me to have photographs taken.

When the police interviewed Maxine, she told them it was a girl called Sharon from the Blythe Jex School. The school had a notorious reputation for children that were badly behaved and were constantly in trouble for bullying and being violent. Maxine told the police that my attacker had taken a comb and scratched her own face to make it look like I had attacked her.

I didn't even know who the girl was. But when she was interviewed, Sharon told the police that she had been told by someone that I had called her a "slag". Obviously I had not done that, I was a really shy, quiet girl and would not have made these accusations. I hated trouble and did my best to keep out of the squabbles that invariably took place around me.

The next day I went to see my Gran with my Mum. My Gran was a cleaner for an elderly couple. She was totally shocked when I walked in with my Mum. Gran hurried off to get one of her employers.

The elderly gentleman came in and asked me to sit down. He closed his eyes and gently put his hands over my eyes. I immediately felt a strange tingling feeling and a massive amount of heat coming from his hands. I started to feel a lot calmer, but I did not understand what was happening, or why the gentleman was touching me. I asked my Gran what had happened and she told me that Mr. Duffield was "a healer", I didn't understand what a healer was and when I questioned my Gran she just said that he worked to help people with illness and injuries to make them feel better.

My bruises went down very quickly and even the doctor was surprised at my recovery. I did not realise at the time that this was my first experience of spiritual healing. I wish I had asked my Gran more questions, she never spoke about spiritual matters, but from spirit she has told me that she was a believer..

The court case was heard months later. The police had taken black and white photographs, so my injuries didn't really show up. Sharon was let off with a suspended sentence. My injuries were horrific and I suffered a permanent droop to one of my eyelids. It seemed so unfair that such a violent act was treated so lightly by the justice system. My injuries and the emotional trauma I suffered far outweighed her getting off and I didn't feel that justice had been done.

This event although at the time seemed like a pointless act of violence was proof that even as a fourteen year old I was being guided by spirit and my intuition. Had I have known what the shaking was trying to tell me, I would not have gone out that day. But if the event had not happened, I would not have experienced the healing, which later opened my eyes to a different world.

Thirty years later I was to have my first visit to the Spiritual Church and I discovered that the Duffield's had been the founders of this. I then found out about the healing side of the spiritual pathway.

In the month of November I again had the same strange experience of the shaking sensation when I had been badly beaten up. It was the 5th November 1975, Guy Fawkes night. All day I felt uneasy and the shaking feeling continued.

As a teenager in the 1970's we did not have the distractions of computers, mobiles phones or Xboxes. The TV programmes were not very good, so we were all looking forward to the bonfire night display and the following party. I got myself ready and the strange feelings that had been with me all day got worse.

There were loads of us at the evening and we were mesmerized by the fireworks. A rather noisy rocket was launched into the air and went high into the sky. We watched with amazement as the rocket started to turn and come back into the crowds of people. Unfortunately the rocket hit a young boy called Paul in the eye. Paul was screaming in pain as he was taken to the hospital.

The next day we were given the news that Paul had lost the sight in his eye and was suffering from the trauma of what had happened. This caused much discussion at the school and left everyone shell shocked.

Nobody could understand how such a lovely evening could have ended in so much sadness. Paul came back to school but where he had always been the practical joker, the experience left him withdrawn and nervous. I don't think he ever fully recovered from the emotional trauma. He had wanted to join one of the armed forces, but due to the disability he had been left with was unable to go ahead with his plans.

My Steps into the Real World

As a teenager, I used to spend a lot of time reading; I was very much alone but found great pleasure in learning. Books were my company and my escape from the real world.

A trip to Guernsey at the age of 15 got me hooked on Agatha Christie murder mystery novels.

My parents used to think I was rather odd for being so interested in these morbid books. But my lovely Gran shared the same interest as myself and over the next few years we read all of the 76 mystery books that Agatha had written.

I liken the work I do today as a clairvoyant medium to being a detective. Through working in this way the spirit world give me the most amazing evidence to prove there is no such thing as death. Each time I work with someone it is as though spirit is giving me the pieces of a jigsaw puzzle to build up into the bigger picture of their life. I believe it is just the physical body that dies, but for me the spirit lives on eternally.

As I continued through to my last year at school, I couldn't wait to leave. I was not academic in any way and struggled with my final exams. The only subject I really loved was English language and literature. As part of the exam work we had to study a play called The Crucible which was based on the works of Arthur Miller. It is the fictional story of the Salem Witch Trials held in the seventeenth century.

I found the play fascinating and although the play was fictional there are plenty of real stories about the events of the Witch Trials which have been recorded through history. My research led me to many stories where witches were accused of being devil worshippers. A lot of them were put on a ducking stool. If they drowned they were innocent, if they lived they were guilty, so whichever way you look at it they were doomed to death. There are so many references to the Witch Trials on the internet and to the Witch Finder General, who was in charge of finding these witches.

The interest in the play later formed part of my spiritual pathway as I became interested in Paganism and studied the subject in detail.

The rest of my school days were quite boring, I busied myself with my books and spending a lot of time on my own, preferring my own company rather than the strange behavior of the people around me. I was relieved when the day came to leave; I knew my exam results were not going to be very good. My poor memory and lack of enthusiasm let me down.

It was a real struggle finding a job that interested me enough; I really didn't feel I was good at anything. I wanted to be a psychologist or a detective, but my lack of grades let me down. I was quite pleased to get a job in an office; this promptly lasted six weeks before I was given the sack. This was to be the first of many disappointments.

I knew that people found me a bit strange, in the same way as my family did. Although I never behaved differently to anyone else! I really couldn't understand why I was unable to form relationships with people of my own age. The work place was an environment that I found difficult to fit into, although I tried to work very hard at the tasks given to me. People just gave me a bit of a wide berth, I know now it was because my energy was so sensitive that I picked up on people's moods, I also found for some unknown reason that I attracted a lot of jealous people around me. Although I tried very hard to get on with people, I was just left feeling very lonely and different!

At the weekends I used to meet up with my friend Sandra. We both worked so we did not have much contact, this was before mobile phones became an everyday piece of equipment. Sandra was the only friend I had; she was very much like me. But Sandra was a bit more of an extrovert and a risk taker. She even rode a motorbike.

I remember seeing Sandra one day it was just after we had both turned 18 by then. We went round to all the shops fitting on posh dresses that we would never have been able to afford in a million years. I fitted on the most amazing dress and even though I was tiny framed, managed to get the dress stuck over my head, I couldn't get it on or off. We collapsed in giggles and eventually I wriggled out of the dress again. The shop assistant came in to see what all the fuss was about, and it put paid to us ever going in that shop again.

When I saw Sandra, I had the same odd feeling that had been part of my life; I felt so anxious and didn't really understand why I was getting this bad feeling again. I didn't realise that it would be the last time I ever saw my friend.

A few weeks later, I had a visit from a girl who I had been at school with. I could not understand why she was so desperate to come and see me; we had not really spent much time together since our time at school. The reason for her visit was to give me some shocking news. My best friend had been killed in a car accident! She was my first loss to the spirit world.

Sandra had been travelling on her way to a party and the car that she was travelling in was unsafe. The car left the road and ploughed into a brick wall. The seat had not been screwed down and Sandra was killed instantly as she hit the roof.

I really had no understanding of the spirit world, or what had happened to my friend. I often think that if I had known what I know now, I would have handled the news of her death better. I could only imagine the trauma her family went through, it seemed so incredible that a girl that was so full of life had met her ending in such tragic circumstances at such a young age. I often think of her but I know that she is okay now. I have more understanding now of why some people do not make old bones and I believe that no one ever goes before their time.

A few months after the death of my friend I started to suffer really badly with the pains in my abdomen that I had been experiencing for many years. Although I had seen many doctors for a number of years, I had never been referred to the hospital. My Mum decided to call out the doctor as I was doubled up in pain and a really nice locum came in. He promptly sent me into hospital.

When I was released my GP was really angry saying "the locum doctor neither had the experience, nor knew you as a patient. He should have realised that you didn't need to be sent to hospital wasting their valuable time". This was the doctor that had prescribed me the tablets that had sent me blind years earlier, so I really don't think he knew me either.

Three months later I was getting ready to go to a party, I started to get the terrible shaking back. I dismissed the feelings and busied myself getting ready to go out. Later in the evening, I

began to feel really ill and was doubled up in pain. I had spent most of the evening in the toilet being sick and it was really late by the time my boyfriend delivered me home.

I got into trouble with my parents who thought I had been drinking. The next day I couldn't move, so Mum called the doctor again. As it was the Easter bank holiday, the inexperienced locum came in to see me. He was really angry that I had not been sorted out by the hospital when he had sent me in before.

As a result of the "inexperienced" doctor, he saved my life. I was admitted with peritonitis caused by cysts on my ovaries. I had to have one and a half of them removed. Because of my age, the remaining half had been repaired and left, they told me that it would be unlikely that I could have any children, but they wanted to leave the remaining half just in case.

It was around the time of Sandra's death that I started my new job as office junior in a firm of accountants. I wasn't particular bright, but I did know my alphabet and this came in very handy as my main job was filing correspondence for the accountants. Although this was very boring, I knew that it wouldn't be long before I was promoted. I had a feeling that the receptionist would be leaving, I don't know where the feeling came from but I imagined her coming in and saying she was pregnant.

A couple of months later, an announcement was made that Linda was leaving to have a baby. I was duly promoted and got paid for a job that I loved doing – talking to people! In my new role, I used to take phone calls and greet clients as they were waiting to see the partners of the firm. I used to find that most of the employees would end up in my reception area and confide all their problems to me. Even some of the clients used to tell me things I should never have been told.

Although I loved my job, I didn't really get on with the girls in the typing pool. They were very stuck up and thought I was beneath them. The lady in charge was secretary to the senior partner, she was even worse than the girls and can only be described as the office bully. She would take any opportunity to tell me off, usually pulling me into the room that the typists sat whilst she shouted at me about how useless I was. Ann was a nasty piece of work and again I had a sense with her that she was carrying on with one of the accountants. She was a married lady but I just had a feeling that she was seeing another man.

One day she came after me shouting her off mouth at the top of her voice that I had made a typing error on an important set of accounts. After six years of putting up with her abuse, I snapped back at her. I told her that she had no right to criticise me when she was having an affair with Gerry. The look on her face was a picture, but I decided I could not stand working for the company anymore and handed in my notice.

Even now when I have people coming to me for readings, I know when they are off work due to the stress of being bullied. Unfortunately bullying is common in the workplace, it doesn't stop when you leave school. I still remember how I was bullied at the accountants and realise that this was just another spiritual lesson that I had to learn in order to help other people. I have learned well the lesson of being bullied, because I now have the perfect job and only have myself to answer to.

Even though I found myself out of work after leaving the accountants, I managed to find a job as a telex operator. I was soon promoted to a different department as a computer operator. I smile now as I am using my lap top, which is very compact. The room that used to hold the disc drives for the computers was a controlled environment. The discs that we used to back up were so large and heavy you needed muscles like Popeye to lift them.

How technology has changed it is hard to believe that so much important information is stored on tiny little pieces of metal.

Unfortunately I had to give this job up just after I moved into my new flat; I had become ill due to the shift patterns playing havoc with my sleep patterns. The night shifts used to really mess my system up, every three weeks I would go for a week without sleep but the job had given me an income so that I could afford to purchase my new flat, so it wasn't in vain.

Moving into my new flat was a whole new experience; I had my independence and the responsibility of all the bills that came with it. It was the first time I had ever been alone and I found it really hard to deal with. The loneliness was a big part of my life I had never felt a sense of belonging to anything or anyone and living totally on my own highlighted this.

The nights were long and I couldn't sleep, I stated to get into a pattern of having a vodka and tonic before I went to bed. This was the time that I started to sense spirit people around me, it scared me and soon I was knocking back a bottle of vodka a day. The quality of my life was not good and the times in my early twenties were probably one of the hardest I had to cope with.

Just after I moved into my flat, my Mum became very ill. She was taken into hospital and underwent an operation. Mum had been booked for a hysterectomy, but the cysts she had weighed 9lbs and she had part of her intestine and bowel removed. Mum was lucky a surgeon that was over from Australia did the operation and because of the training he had, he was able to save most of her bowel. My Dad was so worried; she was in the operating theatre for over nine hours. Dad thought he was going to lose her. He had never been very good on his own and he wanted me to go back and live there so he had someone to look after him. The state I was in I couldn't look after myself, let alone anyone else.

I was much closer to my Gran than my Mum and had spent a lot of my early childhood with her and Grandad. I woke up one morning and had the same awful feeling that I had now become used to having. I didn't understand why I would get these feelings, but I knew that something bad was going to happen. Dad called later in the day to say that my Grandad had been taken in hospital after suffering a stroke

I was distraught and went to see my Gran, naturally she was upset herself. I spent a week with her taking her to the hospital to see my Grandad. We were told that he wasn't expected to survive for more than a week. The stroke had left him without speech but as I went to leave he struggled to say "Goodbye Sally". I am sure Grandad knew he was not going to see me again and later that day I got the news that he had passed over to spirit.

This was a very difficult time for Gran, my Mum had only just come out of hospital and she would not go to the funeral. Sadly Mum had never gotten on with Grandad and she didn't want to go.

I realised that I had to do something about the state I had got myself in, I had no job and the drinking was costing me a fortune. I was really upset one day and I came out of my flat to make my daily trip down to the off license. The door opposite opened and a young man came out. I had never met him before but he smiled and said hello. His name was David and he worked for the RAF which was why he was hardly around. As I got to know him I stopped drinking and soon we were planning to get married.

I didn't realise at the time I bought my flat that I would get a husband thrown in as well! We were both lonely people and on reflection I think that is why we were brought together. Gran was still finding it difficult to cope without Grandad. If I hadn't have bought my flat I would probably have gone to live with her. Unfortunately I added to her stress by telling her that not only was I getting married, but I was moving away to the Mull of Kintyre in Scotland.

David and I got married on the 14th January, 1983 he had to leave for his new posting in Machrihanish two days later. It was six weeks later when I finally saw him. We were waiting for married quarters, so it was impossible for us to live together. I moved up to Scotland a few months later and this became my introduction to RAF life.

RAF life is a lot harder than people imagine because of the nature of the job security is always top on the list. At this time there was a lot of trouble in Northern Ireland. The camp was always on a high security alert. Slowly I got used to my new life style and the fact that life was so terribly different from civilian life. Because of the high risks of the threats from Northern Ireland, each time I got into my car, I had to remember to check it thoroughly in case a bomb had been planted in it.

Six months after I joined David I got the news that I was pregnant. Considering I had been told a few years earlier that I would never have children, it came as quite a shock. It was good news and we were the only couple at that time on the camp without children which made me feel very left out, so I finally thought that I would fit in to this way of life and not be classed as "odd" anymore, I found it very difficult making friends because of the fact that I had no children, this was all the other RAF wives used to fill their time with. Hardly any of them worked, the constant moves made this very difficult.

We had some time away to visit our parents and tell them the good news. Even though everyone was really happy, I had a niggling doubt in my mind that something horrible was going to happen. We had visited my parents first in Norwich and then stopped off in Blackpool where David's parents lived.

I woke up in the morning shaking again, this got worse during the course of the day. We had planned to visit the fun fair and although I was reluctant to go on the rides, I eventually gave in and took the plunge. One of the rides was really frightening; I have never been very good with anything that knocks my balance and I remember screaming in fear. I don't know if this had anything to do with what happened later, but I was woken up with pain in my abdomen. As I got up to go to the bathroom I screamed as I noticed I was bleeding. David came rushing through and called an ambulance. I was taken to the hospital and put on the maternity ward as they told me I was losing my baby.

I had thought that everything would be alright as I had gone several months into the pregnancy, I didn't realise that anything could happen after the first three, I was very naive about such matters.

Sometimes the nursing staff does not seem to have any consideration of people's feelings. I had been put into a bed next to a girl having a termination. Obviously I had no idea of the girl's circumstances, but I was so angry that I was losing my child and she wanted to end her pregnancy. I became so distraught that finally the nursing staff moved me into a different bed. I didn't understand at the time why I had been put in this situation, it seemed so unfair and callous but later in life I was to realise why I had to go through this experience.

When we returned to the RAF camp I was given the news that we had to move out of our three bedroomed house, into a smaller one. I was told that I did not need a large house as I had no children. This really hurt and I had not physically or emotionally recovered from the trauma. The house we were leaving was due to have some major repair work done to it before the next family moved in. I was told that even though the house was to be gutted, I still had to do what was called a "march out". This is where the house is inspected to make sure it is spotlessly clean. If there was any dirt or holes in the wall where pictures had been hanging, you would be charged money to put the house right.

I cleaned the house thoroughly; one of the tricks of the Officer was to look inside the toilet rim with a mirror to make sure there was no lime scale. I cleaned the toilet rim with a toothbrush to eliminate any lime scale. This was common practise with RAF wives, the toothbrush was a major part of our cleaning equipment! David was working twelve hour shifts and unable to help with the housework, although he was a very tidy person, so the cleaning was left to me.

My house was so clean you could have eaten off the floor. It was so embarrassing if news got round the camp that a person had been fined for leaving a dirty house, that I made doubly sure the house was scrupulously clean. When the inspection was done I was told that my house had passed but that I was being given a fine for leaving flowers in the garden! I couldn't see the sense in destroying something so beautiful, but apparently the RAF required the garden to be as sterile as the house.

My life started to change within the camp, where I had started to be accepted because of my pregnancy, this changed. People started to cross the streets to avoid talking to me; I suppose they didn't know what to say. After a few months I was so depressed at having no job or people to talk to, that I returned to England, leaving my husband there.

When I got back to England, I lived with my Gran for a while. I was waiting for RAF quarters to live in. My Gran had moved into a tiny one bedroomed flat after Grandad had died, she found the memories too much to cope with.

One of the reasons for leaving Scotland was that we had financial problems, the fuel bills were enormous and we got ourselves into debt, something that was frowned upon in the RAF. Our cheque book had been taken away until we paid our debts. I had no money to live on, so I was forced to find work.

I managed to get a temporary job in a dentist as a receptionist. One of the ladies was really nice; she had a wicked sense of humour. Her name was Annie, she used to spend a lot of time talking to me about everything and I felt so comfortable with her energy. I knew there was something different about her; she was not like the other people I had been around. But we never discussed anything out of the ordinary, but we did have many laughs.

I left the dentist when I became pregnant again, my husband had finally returned to me after being apart for a few months. Little did I know at this time, that Annie was to be an important connection further down my spiritual pathway.

David had been posted back to Watton the base that he had been at when I met him. Our debts had been cleared and we were given back the cheque book. My pregnancy was a bit of a nightmare, I was constantly sick all the time; I thought that women were supposed to glow when they were pregnant. I had lost so much weight I looked positively ill.

One day there was a knock on the door; I struggled to open it as I was so poorly. A lady stood there selling lucky charms, she was a gypsy. She asked if she could sit down on the step as she was tired. I got her a glass of water and sat next to her. She took my hand and looked at my palm. She told me that I was going to have a baby boy soon; even though I was four months pregnant I had lost weight and it didn't show, there was no way that she could have known this. She also told me that my life was going to be turned upside down, that we had to move and we would live by the sea. She told me I would have two husbands and three children. She said later in life I would be called upon to do work with spirit and that the latter part of my life would be more settled.

I found the words I had been given very frightening, David had only just been posted back and there were no RAF bases by the sea! I didn't understand what she was saying about two husbands, I was happy with the one I had got.

A few days later, we went into the local town to hire a television. I was really bored at home and wanted something to fill my time with. The shop was obliged by RAF law to let them know that we had done this, so that the TV license could be sorted out. Two days later, David came home from work really upset. He told me that the RAF had thrown him out for "financial irresponsibility". Although we had no debt, the officer in the RAF had said we could not afford to have a child and it was bringing the reputation of the Queen into a bad light.

We were thrown out of the RAF quarters and ended up living with David's parent in Blackpool. The gypsy had been right with her predications. Although David's parents were lovely, I hated living so far away from mine, they couldn't see their Grandson, so I made the decision to return back to my parents just before Adam was a year old. My parents were so pleased to celebrate his first birthday on the 17th April 1987.

David eventually came to live with me at my parents, but they didn't get on and we were forced to move out. After spending a few weeks in a grotty B & B, the council rehoused us into a place that was miles from anywhere. Just after Adam was born I found myself getting very low, I didn't understand about post natal depression and I began to comfort eat. This was a pattern I had adopted each time I was unhappy in my life. My down fall was cakes, even though we did not live near a shop, the bakers van used to come round twice a week and I would buy a box of six cakes. I used to eat three or four and because I knew my husband would be angry, I used to hide the rest by eating them and burning the box!

I finally started to feel better in myself and joined a slimming club. It was a four mile walk, as I had no car, but I used to make sure I walked it every week to get weighed. I finally lost the two stone I had put on,

My second son Sam was born on the 18th July 1989, we were given another house in Norwich. I didn't have a car and I couldn't get any shopping. Also we were the only people in the village to have children, very strange after the reverse in the RAF. All of the people were elderly, so I was pleased to be able to move nearer to my parents.

After Sam was born, I contracted a virus and became very ill. I was diagnosed with Rheumatoid Arthritis. When Sam was six weeks old David left me as he could not cope with family life or my illness. He came back for a short while only to leave again to pursue his career as a children's nurse.

Little did I know this was to be the start of my spiritual journey. The boys had gone to see their Dad and some friends took me to my first ever psychic fair. I was amazed; I had never experienced anything like it. I had my tarot cards read and was told that one day I would help people by teaching them. I thought of my school days and how much I hated them, I found it hard to believe that I would be teaching children. Obviously they were talking about me being a spiritual teacher, which happened many years later.

One day I came back from my walk to take Adam to school, the journey was up a steep hill. I was in agony and the next door neighbour, who was in the garden, spoke to me. He said "I have seen you struggling with your walking, I do Aromatherapy Massage and I would like to help you. If you let me massage you, I am sure I can help you to feel better and get you walking again". I agreed and spent the next few days in absolute panic at the thought of taking my clothes off in front of someone. I had become very depressed and had put on a lot of weight.

I finally had my massage, I was so stressed about being naked and had spent all day worrying about it, I nearly didn't go. My worries were unfounded; I undressed in private and had a towel over me.

The massage was so relaxing and I began to have them regularly. They helped the pain and also my over-eating. I had been given anti-depressants by the doctor a few weeks earlier and the combination of the two helped me to shed nearly three stone in weight.

I began to feel confident in myself and booked myself on to the massage course that my neighbour Bill had done. I was so impressed with the way it helped me, I just knew I could help others by using it on them.

I had started to have a relationship with a man that I had worked with before I was married and the bizarre way that spirit brought him back into my life was very synchronistic. I had originally met him when I was twenty years old. He was made redundant and had to move back to his house in Nottingham. I had visited him a couple of times but then lost touch and got married.

One day when I had begun to feel better, I had this thought that I needed to ring him. I decided to try his old telephone number in Nottingham. I do not know to this day how I remembered it, my memory was not very good, but I did. His Dad answered the phone and to my surprise he remembered who I was. He told me that Rick had moved back to Norwich as they didn't get on. He told me he was living in Primrose Road; I was living in Primrose Crescent, which was the other end of the suburb. I could not believe how strange this was.

What was even stranger was that I went into the local supermarket a few days later and bumped into him. Rick said "you've been busy" nodding at my children. I gave him my number and he said he would call me. We started to see each other regularly and go out for meals; he helped me with my garden and used to buy me plants as he knew I was broke.

A few months later, I got up one morning and started to be sick. It continued for a couple of weeks until it dawned on me that I was pregnant. I did a test and to my horror, it was positive. I was really distraught and I called Rick to tell him, his reply was "is it anything to do with me?" As you can imagine, my response was not polite. I was embarrassed that at the age of 32 I had found myself in this position, I should have known better. Rick came round to discuss what was going to happen; he told me that he could not be a Dad.

He had no intentions of being a part time Father and I knew that I couldn't cope on my own with another baby. I was finding it hard with the having two children under the age of six. I had very little money to live on so I had to make the heart rendering decision to have a termination. It was not something that I believed in, but I felt there was no choice.

The date was booked and I found myself waiting to go into the operating theatre on my own. Rick was nowhere to be seen, he had decided it would be best if I was alone. As I was waiting to go in, I thought about the years before when I had lost my baby and how the girl next to me was terminating hers. It made me realise that not everything is as it seems at the time. My termination was done on the 14th February, Valentine's Day. It is a date that used to haunt me up until a couple of years ago, when I learned to forgive myself.

A few days later, I felt really depressed. I was so alone again and I didn't dare tell my family or anyone else about my experience for fear I would be judged as a bad person. I was driving down the road and at the bottom of the hill was a set of traffic lights. I was crying uncontrollably and the thought that went through my head was that even if the lights had changed to red, I wasn't going to stop. I suddenly felt a wave of calm come over my body and was surrounded by a sense of peace. As the lights turned to red, I stopped the car and lived to tell the tale.

I didn't realise at the time that what I had experienced my first contact with an angel. I have experienced this feeling many times since and I know it is my Guardian Angel looking after me. There are many books full of stories about angelic experiences.

A New Spiritual Way of Life

The day that I was in hospital was to be the day I started my massage course. I had to put it off for a few months until the next one was held.

When I finally started the course, I thoroughly enjoyed it. I had studied lots of books about aromatherapy and massage. The course was amazing and we learned many things about energy and colours. I had my first experience at meditation and I felt so much better in myself.

I completed my course which took me several months as it was held over four weekends. Before I took my final exam, I had to do over 100 hours of practise massage. I really enjoyed relaxing people by using the oils, my clients were left with not only a sense of peace, but they were pain free.

One of the things I learned on the course was how to manifest things into my life. As part of the theory we had to design a treatment room and write down everything we needed to carry out our work. We had great fun designing it, coming up with beautiful candle lit rooms, nicely decorated to provide the relaxing atmosphere we were trying to create. We planned where the furniture would be and the layout of the rooms.

There were twelve students on the course that did the designs the tutor looked at each of the plans and asked us all what we had missed off? We looked at our plans again, very bemused and could not find what was missing. The tutor pointed out to us that we had all forgotten to put in electric sockets. A big lesson was learned by all, not to forget any of the details when you are manifesting.

Whilst I was practising, I learned to massage on the floor. Therapy beds were very expensive then and I could not justify spending hundreds of pounds on one. I did a manifestation list and put the table on the top of the list. A few days later one of the Mum's at the playgroup mentioned she was getting rid of her therapy couch. I asked how much she was selling it for and she told me I could have it in exchange for a couple of massages.

I was thrilled; this meant I could offer my clients a proper bed to lie on. We were not allowed to charge people until we were qualified but we were allowed to accept donations and gifts. I used to work on a farmer and he brought me wonderful fresh vegetables that he had grown on his farm.

The week before my final course I was short of thirty pounds for final exam. This was the amount of money I had to live on, it had to pay for food and all the bills as well as clothing etc., I was dreading that I would not be able to take my exam, but I kept hearing a voice urging me not to cancel it.

The night before I was due to take it; I had a young trainee doctor come for a treatment. He asked me how much he owed me, but I explained I was only allowed to take donations. He went back upstairs to put some money in my box and told me he had made a small donation. One of my ladies used to donate 10p for her massage which seemed a lot of hard work and didn't even cover the cost of the oils I was using. But without my certificate, that was how it had to be.

When I went back upstairs to empty my box, I was shocked to find that there was £30 and 10p! It was the amount I needed to pay for my final exam. I was right to trust my intuition and not cancel it. The work has never been about the money, but we do have to live and pay for our learning.

Apart from learning massage, Jenny the lady who taught us, had a library of books we could borrow. The first book I was attracted to was called The Celestine Prophecy by James Redwell. This book made such a difference to my spiritual life; it shows the synchronistic events to find copies of what is known as The Manuscript. It is a fictional book that tells the story of a spiritual journey and people learning how to be more aware of their surroundings and the energy of people. I have read this book many times and still learn something each time. I would thoroughly recommend it to anyone on their own spiritual journey.

My thirst for spiritual knowledge led me to read many different books and I cannot write my own without mentioning the other ones that really helped me tremendously.

As part of our massage course we had to learn about the different body types. Ken Dychtwald wrote a fascinating book called Bodymind. He studied the way that people carried their bodies and the size and shapes.

These different body types all held emotional trauma and it was possible to see by the shape of a person which emotions were being held on to. I found this a godsend and started to look at the shape of the bodies of people around me. It is possible to read a body's part and trauma by looking at the outline. Certain parts of the body can be split into two halves, so the body looks like two different people.

One of the most prominent being a person who has very skinny, under developed legs, yet the top half is heavy and cumbersome. To look at them they look like the shape of a wine glass. People with this body shape usually have the weight of the world on their shoulders. There has quite often been bereavement that has not been dealt with.

Ken Dychtwald found that he could release all of the emotions held in the physical body and eventually change the body shape.

The other book that I find really helpful is by Louise Hay, it is called You Can Heal Your Life. Louise talks of how unresolved emotions can lead to physical disease. This is something that has been a lifelong study for me both of my personal illnesses and that of other peoples.

One of the things I find most useful is to use manifestation to get the things I need to have. I had already experienced this on my course and with my massage couch.

I hated the house which I was living in; it was not a particularly nice area and was opposite a petrol station. My youngest son suffered with Asthma and I noticed it got worse when the pumps were filled with petrol.

I did the list of everything I wanted my new home to have. The things that were most important to me were a large garden, inspired by my Grandad. I loved working in the soil and watching things grows. I wanted to be in the country, but close enough to shops and facilities. I also requested gas central heating, but I wanted a coal fire as well. I needed a spare room to work from, so that I could continue my massage.

I completed my list, put it in a book and promptly forgot about it. At the time I was living in a council house and moves were virtually impossible.

This particular stage of my life was filled with gloom and depression. The depression was caused by my lack of money.

I really struggled from week to week providing for the children my youngest son was old enough to go to playschool, but there was no spare money.

The playgroup advised me to contact Social Services as they would sometimes help with people on benefits. I was fortunate enough to be given help from them. It meant that I was appointed a Social Worker, called Beth, to give me the support I desperately needed.

Beth used to come and visit me from time to time. It was coming up to Christmas and there was no spare money for presents for the boys. I knew that my parents and Gran would buy them some, but I still felt guilty. I was still struggling to pay back debts after my failed marriage and had a gas and electricity meter that not only gobbled money, but were set to take back extra to clear the debts. After everything was deducted, I had only £30 week to live on.

One day, just before Christmas, Beth arrived laden with presents for the boys. I didn't know what to say, I was so pleased but felt guilty that I couldn't cope. I had never found it easy asking for help and felt bad for being in this position. I told Beth how awful I felt for being such a failure. She looked at me, but her arms around me and said "Sally, never be afraid of asking for help. You may not be able to pay back the people that have helped you, but one day you will be able to help many others". At the time her words didn't make any sense to me, but I know now what she meant. I have gone on to help thousands of people since I have been on my spiritual pathway. I have a feeling that Beth was a very spiritual person herself, I often wonder what happened to her.

In April 1992, I received a phone call from the Council offices. They told me that they were offering me another home. I went to look round and was amazed to find that had everything that I wanted. It was in a small village, but was close to the shops. It was in the process of being renovated and gas central heating had been installed, but as I looked through the window I was delighted to see that a fireplace had been left in the dining room and there was an open fire. I went home and found the list that I had done previously and found that I had manifested everything on the list.

The Hardest Years

I moved into my new home in May of 1992. Little did I know that this was the start of what would be the hardest thirteen years of my life.

It didn't take me long to settle into my new home and I was enjoying country life. For the first time in my life I started to make friends and life seemed good. My thirst for spiritual knowledge was growing and I started to study astrology. I learned how to construct birth charts for people. Considering I was not very good at maths, I was disconcerted to find out many mathematical calculations were needed to work out the ascendant and planets.

As a single Mum life was quite difficult and although my parents were very supportive looking after the boys, it was had to go out. I made friends with another single Mum and would quite often look after her children and vice versa. The boys all enjoyed playing together and life didn't seem quite as difficult anymore.

My friend had a date and I offered to look after her boys. She came to pick them up later that evening and brought her new man with her. He seemed to be a very nice person, although she said he wasn't her type.

Eventually she got fed up with him and he started to come and see me instead, we got on really well. He used to stay with me sometimes, a few months later I found out that I was pregnant again. I remembered how I had been told that I would never have children, this time I was delighted. I thought I had found the perfect man, my dream home and my spiritual pathway.

I never imagined it would go so terribly wrong. After I discovered I was pregnant, my partner stopped me from doing the massage. Although it was perfectly safe for me to continue, he said I was not allowed to. The only thing I had to be careful about was the type of oils I used, some could cause miscarriage. But I respected his wishes and stopped my work. My pregnancy was quite traumatic, although I didn't experience the same level of sickness, the arthritis got worse. My mobility suffered and I was tired all the time. My joints really ached and I started to suffer with pins and needles in my left arm and leg.

The doctor could not understand it; he said normally arthritis gets better when you are pregnant, not for me though. When I was seven months pregnant, I was rushed into hospital with a suspected blood clot. Instead of being put on a maternity ward, I was put on a geriatric medical ward. It was really stressful and they put me on blood thinning medication. They assured me that it was safe to do x-rays, even though I wasn't happy about it. I was finally let home a few days later.

My daughter was born at 11.45 on 4th November. I remember the GP coming in for a routine visit. Rather than ask me if I was alright, he was more concerned about if I had a good view of the fireworks form the labour ward ten floors up!

My partner had two children from his previous marriage and I would often look after them with my own two. So with the new arrival there were five children under the age of ten! My daughter had been born with an ear infection and was put on antibiotics at two weeks old. She used to cry all the time as she was a sickly baby. I had been used to having babies that slept all night from a couple of weeks old, so I found it so stressful to not get any sleep myself. It wasn't her fault that she was ill.

The week before Christmas I fell on the ice and broke my arm while I was putting out the wheelie bin. I knew that I had all the children over Christmas and was wondering how on earth I would cope.

My partner changed as soon as my daughter was born and I noticed that his mood swings were getting worse. Christmas day arrived and I did my best trying to peel vegetables and prepare a cooked meal for everyone, despite my broken arm. He was in a really bad mood that day because he wasn't happy with the metal detector I had bought him for Christmas, it wouldn't work and he was shouting at everyone.

My partner wanted to take the children to the fair but my daughter still had the ear infection and was very ill. He insisted that we went and that I was being difficult. I refused because I didn't want my daughter to get cold; I knew it would hurt her ears if this happened.

He became more and more argumentative, all of a sudden he head butted me, I was holding my daughter and nearly dropped her. He shouted at me to stop hiding behind a baby. I was so shocked I didn't know what to do, I was bruised and bleeding. He looked at me and started to cry, the start of many crocodile tears, saying he was really sorry.

Little did I know that this was the start of thirteen years of physical and emotional abuse. I blamed myself thinking I was a bad person, I felt like I was going round the twist, reinforced by my partner constantly telling me I was. After Christmas, I phoned his Mum to tell her what had happened and say that I wasn't sure what I had done wrong. Her words were "oh no, not again" I realised then that there had been a history of this in his other relationships.

The health issues I had started to get worse and I became very tired, my daughter continued to wake several times a night which added to this feeling.

My partner decided to become self-employed and I became a prisoner in my own home, as he was always there.

All of my family knew what was going on, but I was unable to ask them for help. I was very frightened at the violent outbursts and felt powerless to do anything about it. As a result of this I started to comfort eat, my body's way of escaping and the weight began to pile on again, making me feel ten times worse about myself.

The only time I was allowed to go out on my own was to see my lovely Gran. I was really close to her and used to enjoy spending time with her. Every time I saw her, I took her favourite flowers, peach carnations.

When Katrina was ten months old, Gran went into a care home for a short holiday. My partner's children were staying with us and helping in the garden. I wanted to go and see Gran with the children. He reluctantly agreed but told me I could not take my eldest son Adam, he had to stay and help his step-dad along with his step brother. My partner never let me leave the house with all three children; he feared that I would leave him, so he used this as a way of controlling me.

I bundled the other three children into my car and set off to see Gran. She was really happy to see us, but asked where Adam was. I told her that he had to stay behind with my partner; she was very annoyed as she didn't often get the chance to see her great-grandson because of school. I told her that I would pick her up the next day and she would be able to see all the children.

When we were chatting, we looked up and saw Katrina take her first steps. My Gran was so happy to witness this amazing event and her face beamed as she smiled. Soon it was time to go,

Gran's dinner was ready. She gave me a hug and a kiss and shoved a £5 note in my hand. My Gran was the most generous person I had ever met. Even though she was always short of money, she always gave me something before I left.

I woke up the next day in a really happy mood; I was going to collect Gran. I started to get dressed and my partner came upstairs and told me to sit down. I told him I was late and didn't have time, but he shouted the words "your Gran is dead". I couldn't believe it until I rang my Dad and he told me that Gran had passed of a heart attack in the middle of the night. I was beside myself with grief. I loved my Gran so much and now she was gone forever.

At this time I had not explored the Mediumship side of my pathway, but I think if I had understood more about it, I would have been able to handle it a lot better. In my mind Gran was gone and I would never be able to see or speak to her ever again. My understanding of Mediumship didn't come until a few years later.

To this day, my eldest son is still upset that he didn't get the chance to see his Great Grandmother before she left us.

The only memory I have of the funeral is every one going up to my Mum and saying how sorry they were, no one spoke to me. Inside I was being torn apart, I was the one who was closest to her, and my Mum never had the relationship that I did. Although Mum went and did Gran's shopping, she saw it as It as a chore and said Gran complained about everything.

She was never close to Gran, but this was due to Mum's upbringing. My Gran's first husband went off with another woman. When Gran remarried, Mum lived with Gran's best friend. It was during the war and Gran and Mum had stayed with Hilda as my Gran had to work to keep Mum. Just before Gran remarried, Hilda's daughter Joan was killed when a bomb fell on the factory she worked. When Gran was going to move out, the doctor begged my Gran not to take my Mum away from Hilda, he feared she would not be able to cope and she had treated my Mum like her own child. I know Mum always felt rejected and when she went to live with Gran she didn't get on with her Step Dad, who was not used to having children.

I know things were difficult for my Mum as she felt that she was not wanted, but my Gran loved her, it was just circumstances that prevented them from having the close relationship they should have had.

This particular day, I just felt so sad and I thought that it was all a big farce, Mum pretending she was upset, when I knew deep inside she was not bothered. When we had gone to order the flowers Mum had said quite harshly "if it was left up to me she wouldn't even have a funeral".

This caused a rift between Mum and I, we never really had that closeness that I had experienced with my Gran. Although I still went to see my parents our relationship was very distant and I went for long periods of time not seeing them.

Gran was always the peace maker between Mum and I, we clashed regularly. When she went, things were never the same. This was such a difficult time; I no longer had anyone to talk to, although I never told Gran about my violent relationship. But I always knew I could escape to her if I needed to.

The relationship with my parents became even more distant. Although they used to have the boys regularly, my partner would never allow them to look after Katrina. Eventually my partner caused so much fuss that even the boys were not allowed to see them.

I understand so much more about the emotion's my Mum felt, we have talked about it and I see it from Mum's side now. She really thought that my Gran didn't want or love her, but I have told my Mum that she really did. My Mum's biggest problem is that there are lots of questions that are unanswered, but Gran was a private person and I have explained that maybe it was difficult to talk about the things Gran herself was experiencing.

My relationship with my Mum and Dad is much closer now, as I have reached more of an understanding about the past and even though they still do not understand my work, I hope one day they will come to understand me and my job better.

Sometimes we judge people and what they do, but this is one of the most important lessons we have to learn along with forgiveness. When you are made aware of both sides of the story, you view things in a different way. As a result of the many experiences I have had, I am able to do this now.

The Two Worlds Connect

A year after Gran passed to spirit, I was still very down. I felt that part of me had died with her and I could see no way forward.

My relationship was going further down the slippery slope, heading for the bottom. I struggled with everyday life and my confidence had reached an all-time low. I found my partner's energy totally draining. Through my understanding, I realised he had many unresolved issues of his own. His own Father had died when he was four years old, and he had never got over it. His bursts of anger were becoming more and more frequent; his anger was directed at me. I tried to help him resolve things, but nothing would work and I had to get away from him.

I was reading the paper and noticed a body, mind and spirit fair being advertised that day. I had secretly booked a few days away for myself and the children in a caravan. A voice kept telling me that I needed to look round the fair.

As I wandered round, looking at the different stalls and readers, I was drawn to a lady working with Tarot Cards. I went and sat down and she asked me if I had a piece of jewellery I could let her hold. I was very intrigued and asked her what the purpose of it was as I thought she would be using the cards. She explained that by holding something metal, she would be able to get a lot of information from it.

I later found out that this was called psychometry. This term was coined by Joseph R Buchanan in 1842. It comes from the Greek word "psyche" meaning soul and "metron" which is measure. By using this method of divination it is possible to pick up on past, present and future events. The objects are said to retain the energy of the person it belongs to as well as previous owners, in the case of items passed down.

I handed the lady my ring, which had belonged to my lovely Gran. She immediately said "you are about to do something about which you are unsure, but you are making a wise decision. I feel this is to do with travelling and you are running away from someone who is holding you back. I have a lady with you from the spirit world who says she is your Gran. She has asked me to give you the peach carnations and is saying she has all the flowers she needs where she is. I have two spirit children with you, a girl who is about ten years old and a boy about four or five. The little boy says you are to stop blaming yourself, he was not meant to be born. If he had been, your life would have been very different and you would not have your daughter. I know you blame yourself every day for the decision you made, but later in life it will become clear why you had to make that choice".

I was taken aback by these words, she had described by Gran perfectly, gave me information about my relationship, and my spirit children. She also told me I was a healer and on a spiritual pathway and that I would meet many people who needed my help.

I felt so inspired by her words and I knew I had made the right decision to run away. I wasn't sure what I was going to do after my few days away, but I was more concerned as to how I would escape without my partner, who I had left in the Antique Centre.

I phoned my Mum and got her to call me and make an excuse that I had to pick the children up early. The boys used to stay with my parents a lot; I knew they were safe with them and out of harm's way. They hated their step-father, who was very hard on them.

I left my partner in the Centre saying I had to pick the boys up. I had given him a lift in my car so he was expecting me to go back for him. I went in and packed some clothes for the weekend. I then called his friend asking him to collect my partner as I had problems with my car. I have never been so frightened in my life, thinking I would be found out.

I was shaking as I collected the boys, who thought it was all rather exciting. We made our journey to the holiday camp. The children were a bit confused that we were going on our own, but they soon settled down.

The next day we had a really good time, but I had something niggling me in the back of my mind. I felt really uneasy and like a cat on a hot tin roof. I was suffering from panic and felt guilty at running away, but I also knew that I needed this time to think straight.

We woke the next morning with the sound of someone banging on the caravan door. My heart sank to my boots as I realised we had been found by my partner. He had seen the information on the computer and was really angry I had run away.

He started shouting at me and threatening me, I finally opened the door and I managed to calm him down by saying that I would go home with him. My peace had come to a sudden end, all of the fears coming back. I knew that it would become even more of a prisoner after my great escape.

A few days later, I woke up with severe pain in my right eye. I had lost the vision in it and a trip to the doctors confirmed it was an eye infection. I was given eye drops, but they didn't work.

Two days after this it had got even worse and I wanted to go back to the doctors, but we were booked into an antique fair and had to leave at the crack of dawn to get there on time.

My partner was angry because I was late getting up and he drove the van like a mad man to get there on time. We were stuck behind a lorry. The road was very bendy and as it was early in the morning, it was pitch black. He suddenly pulled out to overtake the lorry, as we went round the bend I saw head lights coming the other way. He put his foot down and managed to get in front of the lorry with seconds to spare. I felt so sick as I knew we would have been killed instantly had we hit it. This was the first of many lucky escapes and I am convinced my guardian angel was with me on that day.

I was so shaken by the event; I could not believe the stupidity of this man who had no thoughts for his family or anyone else for that matter. The children were all screaming with fright, my partner was laughing loudly.

Our journey continued in silence and I burst into tears as soon as we got there. I was still in a lot of pain and the other stallholders said I should not have gone. They could see that I needed a doctor, but he wouldn't take me. He didn't want to lose any money, so I drove the transit 30 miles back to get to the doctors surgery. The doctor was very concerned and he made an emergency appointment for the hospital for the following day.

I drove back to the fair and my partner was in a foul mood because I had left him to cope on his own. He would never do anything on his own, if I couldn't go; he always took one of the children with him.

My visit to the hospital was very traumatic; they were concerned about my eye and told me I had to see a neurologist urgently. I had been suffering from different problems since my daughter had been born. All of the symptoms showed I was suffering from Multiple Sclerosis, a neurological condition.

Over the next few months I became worse and my health continued to deteriorate, my partner had the perfect excuse for me not being able to leave the house on my own. The home I had loved so much became a prison cell.

Slowly my health started to improve and I was "allowed" to go out again. I found myself drawn to a Spiritual Centre in Aylsham called Holman House. They were holding a psychic supper and I booked to go. My partner put his foot down and I stayed at home. Not realizing that had I gone on that evening I would have met a very important person.

By changing the pathway that had been predestined, I did not meet this person until nearly a decade had past. I often wonder what would have happened if I had made it to the psychic supper. But I understand more now, that everything happens for a reason, even though destiny is pre-set, you can change your pathway you may not meet up with the people at that time, but you will eventually connect with them. In my case it was to be ten years later!

My reading had inspired and intrigued me and I was given the opportunity of attending a spiritual church meeting, with a friend. I was fascinated by the messages and the Medium was a young man called Steven Treadaway. His messages were very clear and I secretly wished I could do what he was doing.

The following week I went back on my own. I was really nervous and sat at the back of the church. This particular night there were two Mediums working together, they were a husband and wife from Scotland.

All of a sudden, the lady looked straight at me and said she had my gran coming through. I was petrified and wanted to run out of the church. She said to me "I know you want to run away, but your Gran is here and giving you a lot of love. I'm being asked to give you a jar of jam from your Grandad. Your Grandad is rolling up his sleeves and getting ready to throw someone out. I know you understand what he is saying and he is adamant about this. I also want to give you the name of Steven".

Although talking to the Medium scared me, I knew it was my Grandparents. The descriptions she gave me were very accurate

Grandad used to pick berries in his lunch break and he would make a delicious bramble jelly. The most amazing message she gave me was that I had the ability to do the same as her! Although it was my dream, I didn't think I would ever have the courage to stand on stage in front of crowds of people and deliver messages.

I went to the church many times and was given the same message over and over, that I had the ability to work with spirit. I also kept being given the name of Steven, and I did not know who it was. But years later I finally found out who Steven was.

Aside from going to the church to listen to the Mediumship, I also had healing, which made me feel much better. I then started to attend a spiritual healing circle, as I wanted to learn how to do it myself.

As my thirst for knowledge grew, I was introduced to the books by Doris Stokes, a fantastic Medium in her day. Her books were about the struggles in her own life and the illnesses she suffered with. She has written several books and I always think these are good ones to cut your spiritual teeth on.

The other person who I was drawn to find out about was Betty Shine, a great healer. Betty also had health issues, but became better when she started to give healing to others. She was told that she had been ill because she was not using her abilities and it was a build-up of psychic energy. This is such a common thing with healers, we don't heal because we are ill, but when we do, we get better!

The Ghost

My partner's business as an antique dealer really took off. Not only did I have the children to look after, but I had to help with his work as well, There were times I had to get up at 4am in the morning to get down to London to buy stock. He would not do anything on his own and quite often I would be awake all night with my daughter, who never slept.

He had a space in an Antique Centre which was very old. The building was renowned for its ghosts I had heard a lot about the "Grey Lady", but I had assumed she was an elderly woman.

One day I was working in the shop and I was sitting having my lunch. The room I was in had just one doorway. As I was sitting up the corner, a lady came in and started to look round. She went out of view so I thought I had better get up and see if she needed some help. When I walked round the corner, no one was there, she had disappeared.

I thought I had imagined it, but the other dealers were talking about the Grey Lady and I found that she was not an old lady, she was a young girl. I had seen my first ever "ghost".

The story of the Grey Lady dates back to the 15th century. It was said that this was the time of the plague and the family that lived in Augustine Steward House had died of this.

After the family had died, the bailiffs boarded the house up, which was the normal procedure after the Plague had taken them. A few months later when the Bailiffs re-opened the house, they found partially eaten bodies. On further investigation, the body of a young girl thought to be the daughter of the household, was found with pieces of flesh in her throat. She had accidently been boarded up in the house and ate the dead bodies to try and survive. Sadly she didn't and recordings of her spirit have been seen in both the building and the alley.

She was given the name of the Grey Lady as she was dressed all in grey. Many people have seen her spirit and I was fortunate to have encountered, although at the time I didn't realise.

In 1998 I attended the body, mind and spirit fair for the second time. This time synchronicity led me to meet up with a gentleman that I had met on my massage course. Jim had retired as a school headmaster and was teaching Reiki. Keen to learn all about it I enrolled on his course to become attuned to the Reiki Energy.

There are several different types of Reiki, but Jim taught the original "Usui" method. The word Reiki stands for Universal Energy. My personal belief is that we can self-heal when we know how to use both energy and shift emotional patterns that have become stuck.

Dr. Mikao Usui discovered Reiki in March 1922 when he had enlightenment on a sacred mountain North of Kyoto in Japan. He started the Usui Reiki Healing Organisation a few months later.

He gave treatments and taught Reiki to others. He began offering teacher training after the Great Kanto earthquake, which created a demand for people to both have and give Reiki.

After his enlightenment he received not only the ability to give Reiki treatments, but he added the Reiki Ideals, three Reiki symbols, the hand positions and the attunement process.

The history and further teaching and learning are available on the Reiki Organisation website. It is easy to learn and can be used on everyone, young or old.

After my attunement I started to use it on friends and family. I found that whilst I was giving treatments, I could pick up messages from spirit. I was not sure how I did it, but my messages were always gratefully received and understood.

Learning this treatment inspired me to do a course in Colour Therapy. I really loved working with people it was fascinating to see their energy change after a treatment. My clients loved it and they felt so relaxed when I combined the colours with the Reiki energy.

By 2001 my weight had ballooned, I had read an article about Hypnotherapy and addictions. I was addicted to chocolate and could be seen eating it as early as 8am in the morning while I was working at the local playgroup. Most people could not understand how I could eat something so sweet first thing in the morning, but I could eat chocolate anytime.

I went along for my first session and it changed my life completely. When I arrived, I talked about my addiction to Susan, the hypnotherapist. She asked me if there were any foods I hated. I told her that I was allergic to oranges and I could not bare the smell of them. My allergy was so bad that if I even held an orange, my mouth would tingle painfully.

Susan relaxed me into a deep hypnotic trance and made the suggestion that every time I went to eat chocolate, my mind would believe I was holding and eating an orange.

I was so impressed at how it worked and the fact that it was effective. The results were amazing and after a few sessions not only had the urge to eat chocolate gone completely but I could not even bear the smell of it. When the children ate it in the car, I had to have the window open.

I decided this was the next therapy I would learn. I completed a course in Hypnotherapy and qualified in 2003.

I started to work with people helping them with stress, anger management, and eating disorders and giving up smoking. I really felt I was doing something worthwhile.

As part of my studies, I had to do a module on past life regression. I found this really interesting and wanted to find out about any lifetimes I may have had. I really struggled for a while as I could not get my head round the fact that people were re-incarnated, yet we could access them in the spirit world.

The more I researched, the more I began to realise that there are many different levels in the Universe. My personal belief is that spirit are held on a level whereby we can continue to have contact with them eternally and get evidence of life after death. I also understand the soul can be re-incarnated many times which is how we can access the past lives as well.

My relationship had reached crisis point and I was asking for spirit guidance and help. My help came from a knock on the door by my next door neighbour. She told me that my brother was on the phone and needed to speak to me. I asked her what he was doing calling her and she just told me to hurry up. When I picked up the telephone, my brother said that he had a policeman who wanted to talk to me.

The policeman told me that my brother had contacted him because he was afraid for my safety. He told me that I needed to leave my partner immediately. I was really shocked and didn't know what to do.

The boys were going on holiday to Spain with my parents for two weeks, so I only had my daughter to consider. I told the policeman that I would find somewhere to stay. I spent the rest of the weekend panic stricken about what to do.

On the Monday morning I got up and pretended I had a doctor's appointment. I was meant to go to work with my partner. He got really annoyed with me, but I told him I would drive there as soon as I could. I really didn't know what to do, so I called the Citizens Advice Bureau and they advised me to call the council. I spoke to a really kind lady and she arranged for my daughter and I to go into a refuge. Unfortunately I couldn't go in until later that afternoon.

My partner kept calling me as he was getting suspicious, so I packed a few clothes and went to my sister-in-law's house. As I was leaving I saw that my partner had left £2,000 on the mantelpiece. I had no money at all, but I was so scared that he would tell the police I had stolen it, so I left it there. I was really stupid, the money would have come in handy, as I always paid the bills, rent and food I was never left with anything for myself.

I turned up at the refuge which was a very run down bed and breakfast place. I met other women that were in the same position. I had never considered myself to be a battered wife, but reality soon kicked in and I realised it was what I had become.

A social worker came to see me and advised me to go and get advice from a solicitor. I found the details of one that specialized in this field and he said he would put a court injunction on my partner to have him removed from the property.

I stayed in the hostel for two weeks; I had never been in so much fear in my life. I thought he would find me and make me go back to him. Domestic Violence is such a major part of life now, but I do know that there are many violent women who abuse their husbands as well.

I returned to my home, I was still afraid that he would just turn up, but the police fitted an alarm for me in case he did. A couple of weeks later I was getting the children ready to go out and they were in the car waiting for me. I started to shake uncontrollably as I stood in the hall, the phone started to ring. I just knew it would be bad news, so I went to answer it.

I knew that my partner was going to do an antique fair, for the first time on his own. The call was from another stallholder telling me that he had been taken ill with chest pains. I asked if they had called 999 and they said they had not thought of that. Considering the woman was a nurse herself, I thought it was quite strange. They obviously didn't know that we were no longer together. I told them to call for an ambulance.

I knew that someone would be needed to collect his antiques and van, so I called his Uncle. He was really angry because he knew what his nephew was like. He told me he would get the stock and arrange to have it brought back to me.

The next day his Uncle called to tell me that my partner had suffered a heart attack and was asking for me. I really didn't want to see him, but I felt so guilty and went to see him. When I arrived at the hospital he looked so sad and upset and full or remorse for his actions. Against my better judgment I agreed he could come back home. He said he would go for counselling and promised to never lay a finger on me again.

The next few months were much better, but it still wasn't right. We decided to buy the council house I was living in. No sooner than the paperwork was done and dusted, he went back to his old ways. I became trapped in my own home again.

I realised that I had to take my power back and started to go out a little more, when he objected, I threatened I would go back to the solicitor again. I know it was terrible of me I was behaving in the same way as him by control, but I was desperate and didn't understand what I was doing.

Spiritual Development

My new found freedom took me back to the body, mind and spirit fair, but this time as a stallholder rather than a spectator. I guess this was the time my life started to change completely and the synchronistic events that happened put me firmly onto my spiritual pathway, with no going back this time.

I was offering colour therapy to everyone and the lady I was sitting next to was telling me about a development group she sat in. My ears pricked up as she told me the teacher would be coming in over the weekend. I asked if I could be introduced to her and she told me that she would let me know when her teacher arrived.

The next day I had my first meeting with the person I would start to develop my abilities with. I asked Louise if I would be allowed to sit in her group, she told me it took great commitment and dedication to learn, but she was happy for me to attend.

I felt really nervous going along to group for the first time, but I was also excited that I would start to learn about everything. I lived about fifteen miles away, but even that did not deter me. I hated driving in the dark, but I felt it would be worth putting my fears to one side just for an evening.

I arrived at the group and there were about twenty other people who were also learning. We started off with a meditation, it was the first time I had ever experienced anything like this. I felt really relaxed and at peace. I wasn't able to see anything visually in my mind's eye, but I could certainly imagine the experiences the teacher was guiding us through.

Our first exercise was to work with a partner and we had to choose an angel card. The other person had to see what they picked up from the energy of the card. I worked with a gentleman and as soon as I took his card I felt a lot of confusion and emotional pain around him, it felt as though his heart had been ripped to pieces.

I was a bit worried about telling him what I was feeling in case I was wrong, but he confirmed that I had picked up the correct information. I was so pleased that I raced home and told my partner what had happened. He just told me it was a load of rubbish and I was wasting my time!

I couldn't wait to get to my weekly group and each time we would try something different. I gradually began to make friends with people; it was good not to feel "odd" as I had for most of my life. One of the things I really enjoyed was "aura drawings". We were given pieces of paper and coloured pencils and encouraged to draw whatever we wanted to put on the paper. The pictures were then collected in and we were given someone else's to work with. We then had to write down any information we were able to pick up from the energy of the drawing. I cannot believe how much information I wrote down for the paper I had been given, later on the lady who had done the drawing thanked me, I had got everything right.

Although I enjoyed going to the group, I sometimes felt that the teacher was quite hard on me. It was almost as if she was putting me down, she tried to tell me that I didn't know where I was getting the information from and that I was not working with my guides properly. I didn't understand what she was talking about. My experience has led me to believe that we work in the way we are meant to, our Guides link in the way they should. There is no correct way of working with spirit; it is a very individual thing.

The following week we were asked to take along photographs of someone in spirit. The lady who gave me a message from my Grandad looked very familiar, but I didn't know why. There were people that had come from a more advanced group and she was one of them.

As the photographs were laid on the floor, I was attracted to a picture of a young man. As soon as the photograph was in my hand, I started to be aware of the gentleman connecting with me. He became very emotional as he talked about how he passed and gave details about his life. The message was for a lady that had come along; she started to cry as I passed on his many messages. I also became very emotional and had tears running down my face as well.

The teacher told me off and said that I was not meant to let spirit stand that close to me. I had never experienced this before and really did not understand what she was talking about. I never really felt that she explained what happens when you get that spirit contact and in the end I learned to control what was happening, the more experienced I became.

The teacher had arranged a Native American workshop and one of the people who attended was the lady who had given me my message at the group evening. When we were chatting in the lunch break, we realised that we had met at the dentist surgery in 1985. Annie was the lovely lady who always made me laugh. Just a little more proof that synchronicity reconnects you with the people you are meant to be with.

As I became friends with a couple of people from group, one of the girls told me she had never received a message from her Mum in the spirit world. So we decided we would hold a séance with a Ouija board, we arranged to do it round my house.

My partner took the children out; he was very suspicious and didn't like the fact that I was developing my spiritual pathway, so I kept quiet about what we were going to do.

We cut letters of the alphabet out and a yes and no and placed them in a circle on the table. The three of us sat down and started to ask if there was anyone there. The glass started to move about in response to our questions. Then we started to get negative messages from someone called "Raj". The glass was moving frantically round the board and we asked him to go away, but the messages were becoming scarier. He said that he was going to kill us, so we took the glass and smashed it, the board was closed down.

We were all shocked at what had happened and vowed never to do anything like it again.

The following evening we went to group and told the teacher what had happened. She got really angry and said that we did not know what we were doing and should never have attempted it.

A couple of nights later, my young daughter started to wake up very frightened. I sensed a spirit who was being meddlesome. I settled her back down and returned to my room. I woke up a bit later and felt a pressure on my throat; I was really frightened and didn't know what to do. This happened every night for a week.

I made a phone call to another of the girls in the group and she suggested I spoke to Jane, who was experienced in clearing spirits. Jane came round with another lady and asked to see the room. My partner had taken the children out for the evening again, as I didn't want them worrying.

Jane and her friend went up to the room and worked with the negative spirit. When they came down, Jane said there had been a really angry spirit of a young man that was trapped between worlds. He had been killed in a motor bike accident. He had not been able to go over to spirit completely and we had trapped him through the board.

She said to me "I don't know what has happened here, but you have done something you should not have". I explained what had transpired and she told me never to do anything like that again. I assured her I had learned my lesson.

I didn't tell the children what had gone on, but later when my daughter was in the bath she called me in to ask if her room had been healed. I still do not know to this day how she knew that information, but I know that she has the potential to work with spirit like me.

A New Venture

In July 1985, I started to get very bad abdominal pains and a scan revealed that I had got another cyst on the remaining ovary. The doctor referred me to the hospital, but I was told it would be a 20 week wait as the hospital lists were very long.

I was really poorly and woke up in agony on the Sunday morning; the pain was so severe that I had to call the doctor in to see me. He decided the best thing would be to go into hospital as an emergency.

I was seen in the outpatient department and was sent home after blood was taken. I was told again I would be seen in approximately 20 weeks. A few days later, I received a call from the hospital telling me I had to go in for a total hysterectomy on the August Bank Holiday Monday.

When the blood tests came back it was discovered that the marker levels were high, showing that I had cancer. I am sure the angels intervened once more as I was told after the operation that if I had waited for the routine appointment I would not have lived long enough to be seen. It makes me very angry that GP's are not allowed to do blood tests to check for this killer disease, I have come across many people who have found that by the time they got to the hospital, the cancer has quite often gone too far to do anything about.

I had a major operation because of the severity of my condition. I believe that unresolved emotions from past trauma can bring this condition on and I am sure it was because I had not got over the death of my Gran. Cancer eats away at you and the resentment I felt from the family at that difficult time, led to me getting this terminal disease.

Unfortunately I had to miss my development group, but I knew the group were sending me absent healing. Because we work with energy, you do not have to have physical contact on a person to give healing. I am convinced it is why I recovered so quickly. Even the day after the operation I felt full of energy and vitality. It was just my physical body that prevented me from doing anything.

I was getting really bored as I was not allowed to drive, let alone make a cuppa; I was not allowed to lift the kettle! I spent my time watching DVD's, but eventually I got fed up with them. But there were two films that I found amazing, both spiritual in nature. The first one I watched was City of Angels with my favourite actor Nicholas Cage playing the part of an Angel. It talks about freewill and is so very sad. It is a love story about an Angel falling in love with a doctor and using his freewill to become human. I have watched the film many times and each time I learn something else. I think the main message of the story is to appreciate life as you never know what twists and turns there will be. None of us know how long we are going to remain on the earth plane, but the film is a reminder that sometimes we have to take a chance, let go of fear and experience life.

My other favourite film is called Dragonfly and this one is based upon a true story and shows how the spirit world can give us signs to urge us to follow our instinct. In this particular story a Doctor is killed abroad and the spirit world uses children from her hospital to give her husband signs to find her body. This film does have a happy ending.

Tracy, from the group, came to visit me. She brought me some Auragraph pictures to work with that had been done by her work colleagues and family. I worked with all the pictures getting messages and information about the person whose drawing I was interpreting and I had some amazing feedback. Even though I had been seriously ill, I still had my guidance from the spirit world and the opportunity to practise was really good. My life was usually too busy to be able to do much development in this way.

As I was beginning to recover, my partner treated me to an appointment with a Beauty Therapist called Anne. I met Anne about five years previously, but I had not seen her for a year or so. We had a really good natter, each of us telling the other what we had been up to. Anne told me that she had opened a crystal shop with her daughter, but they were going to close it very soon, as they didn't enjoy doing it.

When I got home I spoke to Tracy and we thought it would be really good to take the shop over from Anne. It was a dream that we both had. After a few stumbling blocks, the shop opened in October. I was really happy and it was just what I needed to get me out of the prison my home had become.

Although I was still recovering from the surgery I had gone through some 8 weeks previously, I was filled with enthusiasm and my new venture inspired me. The shop was really lovely and we expanded on the crystals offering beautiful jewellery, oracle cards and spiritual books, in fact anything we thought people would buy. Also it gave people an opportunity to come in and talk about spiritual things, something that it was really hard to do. At this time, there was nowhere to go and discover about the pathway. I had always felt so alone on my journey, now I had lots of people who wanted to know about everything and it gave me the chance to expand my spiritual knowledge.

The run up to Christmas was really busy and we had extended our range of goods to include all of the different spiritual religions. We had Angels, Buddha's, Egyptian Artifacts and also a new range of Pagan and Wiccan gifts. The Pagan goods sold very well and we were constantly stocking the shelves. We had planned to stay open until lunchtime on the Christmas Eve, but we were so busy we did not close until 4pm.

We started to run Mediumship evenings and each month we would have a local Medium do a demonstration for us. Although the shop was tiny, we cleared everything from the middle of the shop to make room for ten people to come and watch. The evenings were really popular and afterwards we would sell lots of our stock.

Just after Christmas I asked our teacher if she would run a development group for us because a lot of people were interested in learning. She decided to do a fortnightly group. This continued for a few weeks until I got a call from her saying she was ill and I had to cancel it. I was on my own in the shop as Tracy had gone to America for a holiday. I did not have anyone's contact details, so I called the other teacher to see if she was available, but unfortunately she was busy. Susan told me to do the evening, rather than letting people down.

I did the best I could from what I had learned and we had a very enjoyable evening. I knew that she had done this with other groups in the past, going away and then deciding to continue much later, it had caused a big rift with a lot of people. It had happened to a healing group that she had taught and when she let them down, the group continued to practise without her. I think it was at this point that I realised that not all spiritual people are indeed spiritual. I would have been more than happy for her to continue the group, but she was so annoyed and showed her true colours.

Prior to her being ill, my teacher had done a reading for me. She knew nothing about my personal life; I was too embarrassed to tell anyone what I was going through. But she picked up that I was like a prisoner and the four walls of my home were my prison! She told me that I would meet a man who would give me the help I needed to escape. She described him physically and told me he was spiritual, but in a different way to me. I was also made aware that he was also a healer.

I took on board what I was told, hoping that the information she gave me was correct. My home life was terrible, but as for meeting such a man, I had no idea where he would be found, I never went out anywhere, other than my shop.

This was a big lesson for me; I thought that all spiritual people were nice. Sadly as the years have gone by, I have reached an understanding that this is really not the case. Spirituality can be a breeding ground for jealousy and back stabbing. I can never understand why, there is so much work for everyone to do, many people need our help and different people need different energies. No-one ever takes anyone else's work away, by spreading horrible rumors and lies it just creates a negative energy. It makes me very sad how so called "spiritual" people behave. There is no room for ego on this pathway.

As the shop was growing, we would sometimes attend Body, Mind and Spirit fairs to promote it. We were booked to attend a fair in Cambridge. As we set up our stall, we watched as some Tarot readers had arrived from London. The fair was really busy and people were just milling around looking at the readers. They were charging £50 for a reading, which was really expensive all those years ago. We had many people complain to us that they could not afford to have one.

I had an idea, I really don't know where it came from, but I told Tracy to put up a sign advertising Auragraph readings. I thought if we got people to doodle on the paper, I could sit and do the readings and they could come back for them later. No sooner was the sign put up; people came and asked if they could do one.

Tracy explained what they had to do and told them to return in about twenty minutes. We were charging people £10 and soon a queue formed that was a mile long! Eventually I just had to do the readings whilst people sat with me, as I didn't have time to keep up with the demand. I really enjoyed the day and it inspired me to do readings from the shop.

As I became busier in the shop with readings, I had extended my work and offered Angel Card Readings as well. It was from doing these that my Mediumship slowly started to come in and I started to sense more people around me. I was covering five days in the shop as well as doing evenings because Tracy still had a full time job and could only cover weekends.

I started to get very stressed as I felt I was doing all the work. Another member of the group decided that she wanted to buy into the partnership. Although Tracy was not very happy about it, I felt that I was the one doing everything and I needed to cut down on the hours. So I trusted the other lady and brought her into the shop.

Unfortunately this caused even more stress as there were three people with their own ideas, so I bought them both out and took control of my shop alone.

I found out a few weeks later that one of them had opened another shop and were running a development group being taught by the ex-teacher who had caused me so much grief. The new shop caused me a lot of heartache; my database of customers had been stolen and soon they were being told that my shop had closed. I cannot say where the rumors came from, but I have my suspicions. Another confirmation, that spiritual people are not always very nice. Fortunately most of my customers were very loyal and supported me until the stress had died down.

I needed some help in the shop and one of my customers, Sue, offered to help me. Sue covered on Thursdays and Saturdays. Sue also taught Reiki and I asked if she would like to do a Reiki group in the evenings. She jumped at the chance and the shop was able to offer more.

Sue was always asking me to come and meet the Reiki group, but my partner would not let me go in. He was always complaining that I spent enough hours in there. It is very strange and although I didn't realise at the time, if I had put my foot down I would have met up with the person I should have linked with at the Psychic Supper a few years earlier. Another missed synchronistic opportunity!

Just before Sue started her group, the shop next door became available. I felt I ought to move into the bigger premises as it would allow us to have a room to do therapies and group meetings. It was perfect for what I needed and allowed me to offer so much more to customers.

Around the Christmas time, just before we moved of the holiday period. Another lady called Nicky came into the shop. She said she had given up her job as a nurse and would love to volunteer. Nicky turned out to be the Mother of one of my daughter's school friends and proved to be an absolute Godsend. I had become more and more busy with the readings and had less time to serve customers.

Nicky also helped me with the groups and Mediumship evenings and also a new group that we were starting about Paganism. Another lady had started the group, but she didn't want to continue, so Nicky and I decided to run it ourselves. I had done a course in Paganism years earlier, so was qualified to do it.

One of the people attending was my friend Annie who I had lost touch with when I stopped going to the development group. Annie still worked full time at the dentist, so she only came into the shop on a Saturday which was my day off. It was good to see her once a month at the Pagan evening.

The months went by and Nicky started to become unwell, so she was unable to help me anymore. My own health had started to deteriorate and I didn't feel I could go on with the shop for much longer. I was doing so many personal readings that my partner started to help out, but this was not ideal as he didn't believe in this pathway, but he was a good salesman and used to sell a lot of stock for me.

Past Lives

One of the therapies I used to offer was Past Life Regression with my clients. I had some amazing cases. From the Hypnotherapy training, I had completed a course in Regression. The Regression course allowed me to gain a qualification in this very valuable technique. I read many books by a gentleman called Brian Weiss.

Brian started as a Hypnotherapist in America. He was working with a client and accidently regressed her into a previous life. He worked with his client Catherine over a few months and found that she had had many past lives. He found he could also get access to spiritual messages from "The Masters" who were from the Spirit world.

I took many people into past life experiences and there were some really interesting facts that came out. Sometimes my clients would say they recognised me from particular past life experiences.

One of my clients called Julie had about seventy past lives. One of the ones she described as being a serving wench in a Victorian Bar in London. Julie was speaking in a deep cockney accent, whilst she was giving me details of the pub. Julie was a Norfolk girl and spoke with a broad Norfolk accent. So it seemed strange to hear her talking in this way.

As she was describing the life she had experienced, which was one of a young girl fighting to survive on the streets of London I was given dates, times and places to check later.

I always feel that our past lives hold the key to experiences we have in our current one. Julie's current life was very hard with little money. She spent long hours working to try and survive. In her past life this was also the case, with little support from family. Again this was a reflection of her current life.

I asked Julie if she recognised anyone in her life as a serving wench that was in her current life. She roared with laughter and said "you are here, behind the bar with me. We have lots of fun and there are loads of blokes eyeing us up". It always seems really strange when clients talk to me of their connection with me in their past lives. We explored many of Julie's past lives and were able to clear a lot of the issues she was holding on to.

Another client who came to me was a gentleman called Brian. He came because he had severe pain in his left shoulder and a fear of heights. Sometimes we carry our fears through into our current life.

When I took Brian into regression, he described in great detail about being a soldier many centuries ago. He described that he was being chased by the men he had been fighting. He had been defeated and tried to run away. He finally ended up at the edge of a high cliff. He had nowhere else to run and the soldier's caught up with him, stabbed him in the shoulder and he fell to his death.

It was clear that this past life experience was the cause of his current fear of heights and physical pain. After his regression, Brian contacted me to say that all his pain had gone and he no longer suffered from his fear of heights.

It is not unusual to find that patterns passed down from past lives are cleared when taken back to relive the experience.

I also had past life experience around thirty years old which I can relate to this. When I was thirty years old I started to suffer from very severe breathing problems. It happened very suddenly and the doctors were not able to tell me why. A couple of years later I attended an evening about this work and was picked out from the audience to be regressed.

My particular experience was not done through hypnotherapy, which takes a good couple of hours, but I was able to access two past lives on that particular evening.

Both the lives that I relived had a profound effect on my life. I described the first life as being a young woman. My father travelled away a lot as he was merchant bringing back fine goods from other countries. My mother went with him on his travels and I was left alone. I became very ill with TB and my life ended at thirty in a sanatorium. My parents could not get back to me and I died alone.

The second life I explored was as a young teenager in France. I had fallen in love with a young boy from the village. My father was very strict and I was forbidden to have any contact with him. We decided to run away together and find work so that we could get married and be happy. We had little money, so we took food and ran away in the middle of the night. My father came after us and he beat me and my boyfriend. I was taken home and never saw my boyfriend again. I was prevented from seeing my true love and lived my life on my own in disgrace. Again I had the pattern of being trapped and lonely.

There were two things that seemed very strange about this. The first being the breathing problems that I started to suffer with in my current life. These problems disappeared after the regression. The second was the fact that I had suffered with physical abuse and was controlled and trapped. A pattern that has emerged from this particular lifetime, with the abuse and control that I have experienced.

I believe we reincarnate with soul groups, quite often there are key people we are connected to this time round. We don't always come back with the same connection and it is possible that in one life you would go through the scenario of being father and daughter, but reincarnate as husband and wife. Maybe this is the connection that I have this time round, but without the other person being regressed also, it cannot be validated. But I have a feeling that the father in my previous life was probably my partner in this one. I also know that the young boy has been connected to me in other lives too.

One of the other memorable clients I worked with was a crystal healer and she used to work in my shop. Janet came to me because she always had a feeling that she was strongly connected to Atlantis.

In the regression Janet described the life she had in Atlantis. She was a healer in the temple which was set up for people to come and receiving healing. She described the interior of the temple that had large crystals placed to give energy and accelerate the healing process. Her life was very simple, there were no worries of money, no greed and everybody was happy. She was able to give details of her life in Atlantis and how it was "heaven on earth". Everyone had their role to play and life was full of joy.

In the temple there were key healers and she described a couple that was prominent in the running of the place. Janet told me I was the Priestess who played in the part of organizing and making the temple run smoothly. I was married to the Priest and we worked together both healing and keeping the temple running smoothly. Janet also recognised other people she was connected to in her current life.

She described how the Atlantian people became greedy, because of this the energy of Atlantis became negative and the temple was closed. Janet said the Priest and Priestess left Atlantis with groups of people. Janet was included in his particular group that went in search of other countries. Janet told me that as they were walking away, they heard an explosion. When they looked back, the Island had sunk into the sea.

This particular regression was very detailed and I felt it gave a real insight into the Atlantian people and the way of life.

There are many articles written about Atlantis, some say it was a myth, others say it truly existed. I will leave you to research and come to your own conclusions on this Island.

A few years later a book was published by Dianne Cooper called Discover Atlantis. When I read it, a lot of the information that was written was exactly as Janet had described. With hindsight, we could have written the story ourselves and had a best seller!

It always fascinates me how people's voices change when they are in their regressed state. My next story always makes me laugh whenever I think of it. I was giving a talk to a group of people at one of the spiritual Churches. I asked for a volunteer to give the members an insight on useful regression could be. My volunteer was a very well-spoken lady.

When I take my client's down through the different stages of relaxation, I take them to the beach of time. I then take them through a doorway and into a bank of fog. As the fog clears, they find themselves in a past life situation.

As I took my lady through the doorway I asked her to tell me what she was doing. Imagine the laughter and shock of everyone as she said "I'm cleaning the bleeding steps". Further questioning gave the story of how she was a scullery maid at the turn of the century, she seemed to spend most of her time cleaning the white steps leading up to the house.

Not all of my clients have had such funny experiences; some of the lifetimes are traumatic and very hard. One of my clients was Pagan and was absolutely fascinated by the history of witchcraft. As I took her back to her former life, I asked where she was and what she was doing. She described herself tied in a chair about to be ducked into a river for being a witch. She was very frightened, but I was able to take her forward in time into another life and she settled down once more.

Sometimes a client does start their regression in a difficult place, I allow them to go naturally into an experience, when they go into an experience that seems very negative, it is usually because something needs to be released. In the case of my Pagan lady, she had a fear of water and had never learned to swim because of this.

I do make sure my clients are completely comfortable and safe. Although they may go through traumatic events, they are not really experiencing it. They just view it as though they were watching a film.

I am always able to return my clients to their current life very quickly, but there was one occasion when I struggled to do this. I had an occasion where I tried to bring back a gentleman from hypnosis and he did not want to come back. His wife was sitting in with him and she became a little worried of his refusal to return to his normal waking state. Eventually I managed to get him to wake up. When he recalled his experiences he told us he was in another world. It was so full of love and peace that he did not want to return back to this life. I wasn't worried about my client, because I know that when you are in a deep hypnotic state the body will eventually go into a normal sleep and eventually wake up. I was more concerned about the fact that my next client was due to arrive in thirty minutes.

My past life regression work seems to come in stages, sometimes I have nothing for ages and then suddenly I get a spate of clients wanting to come. But by the time I left the shop, I was so busy with readings that I didn't have much spare time to worry.

My early readings were mainly working with clairvoyance, and I attracted clients that were usually going through a lack of direction. I was able to guide them through the changes they needed to make. I did not often work with the Mediumship side and I believe we develop at the rate we are meant to. I never pick up negative things and I certainly cannot predict the future. I

merely give people an insight into possibilities that may happen I am given an insight into what is happening around the client's life. I know that people are drawn to my energy because usually they are going through something I have experienced in my own life. Sometimes people just need to know they are on the right pathway, or need to know how to make changes to their lives.

My clients always get healing if they need it, I always know because even now my hands tingle as the healing energy flows through the chakras on my hands. I still enjoy giving people healing even now and quite often I will send them distance healing as well.

Moving Forward

By this time, I was finding it hard to keep up with managing the shop and doing all of the readings, I realised that it was time to move on. I had asked spirit to send me someone to help with the situation.

One day I was talking to a lovely lady called Jane who used to come into the shop regularly. Jane was about to retire from her job as a Psychiatric Nurse and she told me she was interested in buying the shop from me. She was going to run it with a friend of hers. We couldn't continue to run the Pagan group as Jane's business partner was not happy about it. I handed the keys over on Christmas Eve 2005. It was a time of great sadness for me, but I knew I had to change my life. My spiritual pathway was taking me in different directions and owning the shop just limited my capabilities.

I continued to run the Pagan group from my home and I had about twenty members. We used to fit quite snuggly in my living room, but we enjoyed the monthly meetings. A lot of people have misconceptions about Paganism.

The history of Pagans is said to predate all other religions. There are many myths surrounding Paganism. Some people believe it is about worshiping the devil and casting evil spells on people. Nothing could be further from the truth, true Pagans respect and work with the natural elements of earth, air, fire and water. Nature plays a big part in this particular belief and the principle of Paganism is not to harm anyone. They believe that what we give out comes back tenfold, that encompasses good as well as bad. So they will not cause anyone negativity or harm.

Other religions have their four celebrations Christmas, Easter, Harvest Festival and Halloween. Pagans have more celebrations that are known as Sabbats. These Sabbats divide up into what is known as the wheel of the year. The dates differ from other religions and are celebrated in different ways.

The first sabbat celebrated is Samhain, which is better known as Halloween. The date for this is 31st October and is traditionally known as Pagan's Old and New Year. It is a time for honouring those that have passed to the spirit world. It is a good time to contact the spirit world as the veil between the two worlds is at its thinnest.

It is interesting to mention that going back in history, the Catholic Church decided to use the 1st November as All Saints Day. As Pagans already celebrated this day, it made sense to use it as a church holiday. All Saints Day became a festival to honour the saints who didn't have day of their own

Sunset on Samhain is the beginning of the Celtic New Year, the harvest has been gathered and the earth begins to die around us. It is about wrapping up the old and preparing for the new.

The second sabbat is Yule and is celebrated on the 21st December, earlier than the traditional Christmas Day. This is a gathering of families and friends it takes place on the day of the Winter Solstice. It is a festival of the sun and the most important part of the celebration is light, candles and bonfires are traditionally used.

The third sabbat is Imbolc it is the point on the Northern Hemisphere which is the halfway point between the light of the spring and the dark of the winter. It is celebrated on 2nd February. This is also known as the month when love begins and this is where Valentine's Day plays its part.

The fourth sabbat is known as Ostara, the time of the Spring Equinox. It happens around the 21st March when the light is equal to the darkness. This sabbat celebrates the birth of the soil and land. It is known as the time of fertility and abundance because of its close association with the Christian Easter celebration.

The fifth Sabbat is Beltane on the 1st May, which is traditionally known as May Day. This is a day to celebrate fertility and many pagans have a celebration of marriage known as a hand fasting on this day.

The sixth sabbat is known as Litha or Summer Solstice; it is celebrated on the longest day of the year either 21st or 22nd June. The extra daylight hours mean that you can spend more time outside and honour the power of the sun. Some Pagans have a Midsummer's night bonfire which is a time of celebration to bring balance into their lives.

The final sabbat is the seventh one and in known as Mabon or Autumn Equinox, it is in celebration of the harvest and gives blessings for abundant crops, and the gifts of the food from the earth. Pagans also appreciate that the warmth of summer is behind them and the cold of winter lies ahead. It is celebrated between 20th to the 23rd September, depending on the Northern or Southern Hemisphere.

Our pagan group tied in the meetings with the Sabbats so we were able to celebrate them with meditation, food and much merriment

I was happy to continue my work at home and kept myself busy with readings, past life regression sessions and learning even more about spirituality. I broadened my horizons and started to attend more fairs to reach even more people.

Considering how much I hated school, I enjoyed studying and completed a course in EIP which stands for Eliminating Interference Patterning. This particular course taken later in 2006 linked the work I did with the past life regression and the beliefs I had that unresolved emotions cause disease. It is the same way that the colour of our hair, eyes and other physical things are passed down in our genes; we pass on memories and fears.

Many of the clients I worked with had issues about not feeling good enough, lack of confidence and poverty issues. These are all beliefs that can be passed down from the family generations. A person that lacks confidence often suffers this because one of their parents has confidence issues.

One of the things I had to learn to cope with was being able to accept money for my spiritual work. When I had an EIP session the past life experience showed that I was a clairvoyant and killed for my beliefs. It took me a long time before I had studied the EIP to actually feel comfortable charging clients. Although I do not agree with people making obscene amounts of money from this work, I do not believe it should be given for nothing

I work as a full time Medium and have no other income, but I do a lot of charity work and feel that I have a good balance in what I am doing. I am always on call for people and I do not charge for my ability, just for my time.

I was so fascinated by the EIP I wanted to do a follow up one, but it meant I had to go to America as there were no English courses available. I looked on the internet and found the next course was to be held in May 2007, five months away.

Christmas 2006 was one of the many turning points in my life. I had been given a book voucher for Christmas, which I was really pleased about. My love of reading especially spiritual books was still very strong.

I hated Christmas, it was always full of arguments and tears, usually mine and I used to dread it every year. The children always looked forward to it, but as an adult it meant misery for me. On Boxing Day, I drove into Norwich to spend my voucher. I headed straight for the spiritual section and a little brown book caught my eye. It was called The Secret by Rhonda Byrne and explained how you could manifest things into your life. I couldn't wait to get home and read it.

Never have I read a book so quickly, it shows how to manifest the changes in your life that you need to make and it covered all areas of health, wealth, relationships and house moves. I had been working with manifestation since my massage course years earlier, but the book showed you the specific steps you needed to make to bring these changes about.

I started to make a list of the things I wanted to change in my life. One of the things that restricted me was the MS, which left me very tired most of the time. I started to visualize myself feeling better. One morning I got up and had a sore throat and a heavy cold. Normally I would have headed straight back to bed with some aspirin. I took on the suggestions the book gave and started to tell myself I felt better. Within a couple of hours my cold had disappeared, my throat was better and I felt okay again. I have always believed in positive mind thought and I know that by letting go of the negative feelings, a change can be brought about. Sometimes life does take it out of you, but The Secret started to give me a different way of thinking.

After reading the book, I decided that I definitely wanted to attend the course in America, but I didn't have the money. I only had a couple of months to save it and I knew it was impossible. I needed £4,000 to go and I didn't have £4 to call my own. I was positive that with the help of my little book, I would get there.

I emailed the lady who ran the course and told her I was interested. She emailed me back to say that I could have a discount as I wanted to do both of the courses and she knocked £500 off of the price for me. I still needed to manifest the rest as I had to pay for flights and accommodation and food.

When I did the original course, I met a really nice lady called Julie. I knew that Julie wanted to go on the course as well and I told her that if I could raise the money, I would like to go with her. A few days later another friend said that she would also like to come. She told me she would lend me the money and I could repay it at a later date. I already had enough money for the course, but I still needed flight money and to pay for the accommodation.

I knew that I would eventually have the money from a court case that had been on-going for several years, but I didn't know how many more years it would take. It didn't feel right to borrow the money from my friend because I knew she would be constantly nagging me until I had paid it back.

When I got home later that day, there was a message on the answer phone from Julie asking me to call her back. There was only a few weeks left before the course started and time was running out. When I spoke to Julie she said she would put the cost of the trip on her credit card and she didn't mind how long I took paying it back, she even told me that if I could not afford to pay it back, it would not matter.

I couldn't believe that I had received two offers in one day. I knew I had to trust, that was what the little book taught me, so I took Julie up on her offer. I guessed that someone was telling me I had to go, by giving me these opportunities.

At 8am the next morning, I received a phone call from my solicitor to tell me that the company I was fighting had finally made an offer. I was over the moon, I had used the principles of The Secret and it had paid off! I went to America knowing that I could pay Julie back on my return.

The trip was really fulfilling, even though the twelve hour trip was terrifying, flying was one of my biggest fears. But I enjoyed the course and on the way back I did some work on myself to alleviate the fears and the flight back was manageable.

When I returned from America I started to notice changes in the way I worked. I started to pick up more messages from the spirit world. I had always known they were around me, but the energy had started to become stronger the more I worked.

I started to get names of people and new their conditions of passing. I soon began to realise the breathing problems and pains I was experiencing were from the spirit world, not my own and this was their way of letting me know they were around me.

It was at this point that I met a lovely lady called Billie; she had come to me for a reading. She needed some guidance as there was a lot going on around her with her family and work. I gave her an unusual name of a lady and it turned out to be her birth mother's name. Billie didn't know much about her mum as she had been adopted as a baby. By a lovely couple who had brought Billie up as their own daughter.

Billie wanted to ask more about her birth mother, but was afraid of upsetting her parents. I told her that now was the right time to start tracing her family. Billie agreed and said she wanted to do this. I gave her lots of different names which she said didn't make sense at the time, but she was willing to accept them.

A few months later Billie returned and she was really excited. Her parents were happy for her to start tracing her birth family. She had done some research and some of the names I gave her were related to her, but in the physical world, not the spirit world. I told her that she would receive an email around Christmas from her half-sister. I told Billie I felt there were lots of family members she would be able to find. I gave Billie some more names and she went away with the knowledge that she would be able to find her blood family.

Billie came back again after Christmas. She came in with a beaming smile and told me that she had indeed received an email from her half-sister. Although she had sent many messages through Genes Reunited, there had been no reply.

On 13th December she received an email from her half-sister. It is really interesting because when Billie found her adoptions papers, she was adopted on the 13th December, the same day as the important email. She had also discovered that she had other siblings along with nephews and nieces. I told Billie that she would meet them all eventually.

Billie has discovered, with the help of spirit that she has an elder sister, one brother and three half-sisters. Obviously when families find out there is another member that they don't know about, it can quite often cause a lot of heartache. But I just had a feeling it would work out alright in the end.

The next time Billie came she had met up with some of the family members and the day had gone very well. One of the half-sisters had discovered Billie's adoption papers in the loft and Billie was able to find out more information. I told her that there were still some connections to find and over the course of a couple of years, all the family members were reunited. Billie found family scattered all over the country.

Normally I do not see people more than a couple of times a year, but this particular case was an exception to the rule. It is not useful to have readings too often, but Billie had lots of information to find out.

Although Billie's mother had to give her up for adoption, from the spirit world she gave Billie the help she needed to find her family. To me, this is Mediumship at its best, how fantastic to be reunited with family that you didn't know existed.

Some readings I do remember, most of them I forget. I do not believe in keeping records, as I feel this is not for me to do without permission. When my clients come back to me later, I can give them further information. It is when this happens I get the confirmation that what I have said comes true. It is such a privilege to be able to help people and when they come back to say their lives have changed for the better, it gives me a warm feeling and a sense of achievement.

Normally when clients book I only take a first name and contact number, so I don't know who they are or why they are coming. A lot of clients come because they are recommended by others and sometimes I get family members coming as well. I don't feel it is necessary to keep strict records of my clients, but there was one occasion when I wished that I had.

A lady arrived and the appointment had been made by her daughter several weeks previously. I had seen several young girls around that time, so I was unsure who she was when I later tried to find this particular lady. This lady was going through a tough time, as most people are when they come to have a reading. I was able to give her guidance and reassurance that things would work out okay. I asked her if she had any questions. I always finish off my reading by asking this, I don't want to send anyone away until I am sure that I have covered everything.

She said to me "I want to know what happened to my friend" I told her that her friend had gone missing without a trace of her whereabouts. She confirmed this was correct. As I worked a bit more I got the sense that the girl had been strangled and was buried underground. The spirit girl was very frightened and I was made aware that this had taken place many years ago. Again my client confirmed it was in fact over thirty-five years that she had gone missing, but she was unable to give me any information. I was given the name April Fabb and my client looked shocked as she confirmed that it was the name of her friend.

I gave her as much information as I could. After she left, I remembered the day that April had gone missing when I was in the playground in 1969. I did not realise at the time that there would be more connections to April in the future.

I have to say at this point in time, that I cannot guarantee any of the information of the whereabouts of April. As a Medium, there is nothing I would like more than to be able to find out what happened to her so that her family has a conclusion to the mystery.

As a result of this particular reading, I did some more research on the disappearance and found that a book had been written called April Fabb, The Lost Years by the policeman who was in charge of the case at the time. Maurice Morson wrote the book about April but unfortunately it was out of print and I was unable to get a copy until many years later.

My home life was taking its toll again and I was really unhappy and although not quite as much imprisoned as I had been, I felt that my relationship needed to end. I felt in need of some guidance myself and I went to see a well-known local Medium.

I arrived at her home and sat down. She gave me some evidence from my Grandparents which were nice to receive; it was good to know they were both happy and well. She also picked up on my partner and said we were soul mates and would be together forever. I told her that I was not happy with him, but she told me that he was the one I was meant to be with. I tried to explain that he was not a very nice person to me or my children, but she insisted that she was correct. This particular Medium got a lot of information wrong, telling me I had two children, when I quite clearly had three. Plus lots of other things about my family that were incorrect. All though the reading she kept telling me I needed to get a job. I kept telling her that I already had a job, and didn't need another one. But she was insistent that I had to find one. In the end I got rather upset and told her that my work was the same as hers. She said very harshly "but you are not very good, you get all your messages wrong and you should stop seeing people". I was totally shocked and hurt by her words. She then finished by saying "you should find a job you are more suited to".

I left her house trying to hold back the tears. All that kept going through my mind was that I had to stay with a violent partner and I was no good at my spirit work, which was my life.

I started to lose my confidence in my ability and myself. Although I continued to help people, I chose to do more healing than clairvoyance. I couldn't understand why I had been told I was useless at my work when I had so many people come back to me saying things had come true. I know now that it was an important lesson for me to keep my faith and I should have trusted in myself and my abilities, instead I believed this nasty woman.

On the 21st June I had arranged a birthday party for my lovely friend Annie. As the entire Pagan group had become good friends we celebrated her special day with a lovely party.

All of Annie's family came and they brought with them a family friend called John. He seemed to be very nice and had a good sense of humour, but to be honest I didn't really pay much attention to him.

But again another synchronistic event had started to unfold and spirits in their infinite wisdom were working behind the scenes to help me and I didn't realise again. With hindsight I would probably have made more of an effort with how I looked, but the emotional problems I had been going through meant that my weight had ballooned to a massive 19.1/2 stone. Although I was comfortable around my friends, my confidence was low and I knew I looked terrible.

Since the reading I had become even more depressed, so I was not really in the best place for meeting new people, let alone a man. But nevertheless Annie's friend caught my eye with his beautiful blue eyes and stunning smile.

Over the next couple of months my work started to slow down, I kept thinking about the reading I had and thought that spirit were trying to show me I wasn't cut out for this work anymore. I had the occasional clients, but certainly not the quantity I had over the last few years.

In November 2007, I had reached an all-time low. My relationship, despite being told that it was meant to be last forever had started to deteriorate to the point where I need to get away, but didn't know how.

I had reached desperation point and I kept asking spirit for guidance. The depression had got so bad; I didn't know how to help myself. I still kept hoping for a sign from spirit, then one day Annie asked me if I wanted to have a reading. My immediate reaction was to say "no", but my friend insisted that this particular Medium Dennis McKenzie was very good. She said he was really accurate and called a spade a spade and that both she and her friends had been given fantastic information.

I reluctantly agreed to go and the reading was booked for 6pm the following Monday evening. I still had reservations, it was coming up to Christmas and financially I was worried about paying for it. But I convinced myself I could still cancel the reading if I changed my mind.

The day before the reading, I sent the thought out to spirit to say that if I was meant to go for my reading, they would have to provide me with two clients to pay for it. I had a phone call out of the blue asking if a client could come and see me the next day. No sooner had I put the phone down, I heard a knock on the door and a friend was standing there begging me for a reading then and there.

I felt that spirit had kept their part of the bargain by providing me with the clients I had asked for, so I knew I had to go and see Dennis. I started my journey and on the way there I said to spirit that I needed clear signs about my relationship and if I was meant to be on my spiritual pathway. It is not often I ask for things for myself, but I was desperate to have some help. I was still positive that something would shift, but I needed confirmation in stone to get me away from the bad place I was trapped in.

I went in to see Dennis and he gave me a big hug. Dennis works in a slightly different way and he uses numerology in his readings to start with. He told me to give him my date of birth and from that he worked out what my numbers were. The numbers reveal your life path and what type of person you are. It is a fascinating subject and I bought many books about numerology after my reading with Dennis.

My friend has warned me that Dennis was very blunt, but I would never have expected him to be quite as bold as he was. But he does it in such a friendly way that you cannot take offence.

As I sat waiting whilst Dennis worked out my numerology, I felt a wave of warmth come over me, I had experienced this before and knew I had an Angel with me, I think I really needed the reassurance from the Angelic Realm that I was doing the right thing.

Dennis started to say "you are a very sensitive person and are on a healing pathway, you are here to help many people find peace" He went on to say a few more things and then he suddenly said "Oh, I have forgotten the most important number, you do what I do and you are very good. But you are a lazy bitch; you could be doing twenty five readings a week if you wanted. You are so good that you can work anywhere, even in the bog, you are just like me!"

To say I was speechless was an understatement. I know I asked spirit to give me confirmation of my pathway, but even I didn't realise quite how blunt Denis was. That said, Dennis was a lovely person and you really couldn't take offence at what he said.

He continued with some Tarot cards and then said to me "have you found your soul mate? Of course you bleeding haven't. The man you are with is a living nightmare, he is manipulative and controlling. Spirit wants you away from this man and they are going to send another man in to help you. They are telling me if you don't sort it out within eighteen months, it will get messy." He then went on to say that the man I was to meet would help me get away and that I should have met him ten years ago, but we kept missing each other.

I left Dennis full of inspiration for the future ahead of me. Dennis had given me so much positivity there was no doubt in my mind that I was on the right pathway and things would get better. Dennis went on to help the police with the Soham murder and has written his own book about them and his life. Maybe one day I will have another reading with him, but I kind of know what is going to happen these days. Life requires great spiritual trust and when we are completely on our pathways, good things happen.

After my reading with Dennis, my confidence improved and my work started to pick up. Sally-Ann Taylor was back on track.

I owe so much to Dennis, without my reading I would not have had the courage to carry on my work and achieve the things that I have done so far.

A Decade of Waiting Comes to an End

At the beginning of January I had a phone call from Annie. She told me that her friend John was going to be giving a presentation about EFT. I told Annie I did not really want to go. But Annie is very persuasive in a nice way and she pleaded with me saying John really needed some support. He had plans to open up a Centre and wanted to meet people who would play a part in that.

I suppose I went along because it was one of my dreams as well. Some of the Pagan group went along in one car. It was a long drive, so the four of us went along together. My friend Geoff was driving and I sat in the back with my friend Karen, Pammi was in the front. Little did I know it was to be the worst and best night of my life!

When we arrived at the hall, I went to get out of the car, because of my size I could not get out of the back seat. My legs were not long enough to reach the pavement and my rather large body could not turn to maneuver out of the mini.

We were all laughing so much, but inside I felt so humiliated, I wanted to cry. After what seemed like hours of struggling, I told them to go inside. I really thought I was going to have to stay in the car all evening. I really don't know what happened next, but suddenly I was almost catapulted out of the car and I joined the rest of the group in the hall. My friends were laughing about what had happened and we caused a bit of chaos as we were sitting there.

I spotted Annie and she was talking to her friend John, so I went to sit down with the others and waited for the evening to begin.

When John was standing there waiting to start, my heart went out to him, he looked really nervous and frightened. In fact he looked so petrified I didn't know how he was going to be able to deliver his speech.

Suddenly this rather nervous man started to speak; he was shuffling around looking at his feet as though he was hoping for the ground to swallow him up. But all of a sudden something changed in him; I felt his guides were with him, he became more confident in what he was saying.

His eyes were shining brightly, they were a beautiful vivid blue and I was mesmerized by him and what he was saying. As he was talking, I realised that this man was just like me, he held the same beliefs I had. I don't know why but I really felt drawn to his energy. Something inside told me he was really special.

As he continued with his speech, I could not take my own eyes off his eyes. A little voice came out of nowhere and said "you are going to be with this man one day!" I was so shocked at the thought and message I had received, I had never met him before and I was having these powerful thoughts. It was almost like I felt I knew him, even though I did not.

I have realised since that what I was experiencing was a soul connection that had come from past lives. The familiarity of his energy had blended with mine, I am sure he did not feel it. But he was happy to answer the hundreds of questions I threw at him. I couldn't stop talking to him, I felt quite unnerved by what had happened.

So the 23rd January 2008 became the worst and best day of my life. What had started as a really negative experience had ended with a beautiful soul connection.

I suppose the reason I was so drawn to John was because I had never met a spiritual man before and I didn't believe one could exist. The spiritual world seems to be dominated by female energies. I know this has changed now and more men are being drawn to the pathway.

I felt a little bit lighter that evening, I was full of hope and knew I had to do something about my home life and my weight. I had a feeling that the EFT could be used to help me with my issues. I knew that my weight was making me so ill and I had to leave my relationship as I knew it would end up killing me.

With my new sense of enthusiasm I became very busy. I suppose my reading with Dennis had lifted the negativity and I had started to create positivity into my life again.

At the end of January, I attended a Mind, Body & Spirit Fair. One of the ladies did a talk about Image Therapy. She explained by using the right tone of colours, and style you could look slimmer and younger.

I had accepted that I was fat and that wasn't going to change, I had tried every diet going. So I made an appointment to see

Claire Bunton as I wanted to make the most of myself and have a bit more confidence.

My first consultation with Claire was about wearing the right colours for my skin tone. She explained that the shades were so important; there were two types of skin tone cool and warm. I was a cool type so certain colours like orange wouldn't look very good on me. As she draped the different coloured fabrics around my neck, I began to see the difference between the right and wrong shades. The colour that suits me most is Turquoise and the worst one is Black.

Claire gave me a colour swatch to go shopping with and also to see if I had anything in my wardrobe that actually suited me. All of my clothes were baggy and dark, an effort to hide my ample figure.

Claire said the best colours for me were light and bright and she told me it was more slimming to dress in head to toe white, than in black.

I went shopping and bought a few different tops, I knew I wanted to lose weight, but I needed to do something immediately. As I started to wear the right colours I became more confident.

I had a further appointment to revamp the style and shape of my clothes. The baggy tops and leggings just had to go. I really didn't realise how awful I looked and I cringe when I see old photos of myself. Claire said for my body shape I needed to wear knee length skirts and dresses. I was horrified, my legs resembled tree trunks. But I decided anything was worth a go, and this lovely lady was the expert. Claire also recommended lower necklines. I had a more than ample bust and a large tummy to match; my partner certainly wasn't going to allow me to show the slightest bit of cleavage!

Claire said I needed to have a good fitting bra to give me support; apparently underwear is just as important as outerwear. She also recommended empire line dresses, which fitted under the bust but the looseness would cover my stomach.

I had told Claire all about my work and she had asked me for a reading. I picked up that Claire would have children and that there was a miracle going to happen in December. Claire didn't understand what I was talking about but I told her not to worry.

Claire had mentioned that she was starting a slimming club as she could not understand why she had put on a lot of weight. A few weeks later Claire phoned me to say she had discovered that she was 26 weeks pregnant and the miracle would arrive in December! Claire gave birth to a beautiful bouncing boy and both Claire and her husband were delighted. It just goes to prove that miracles really do happen.

I was so grateful for the help that Claire gave me with my image as I had started to work more in the public sector so I took on board the ideas she had given me and it literally transformed overnight. I gradually changed the way I dressed and as I did my partner became more aggressive and tried to put me down even more. But I stuck to my guns and felt a lot better for it.

Moving Forward, with a Special Spirit

I knew that one of Annie's dreams was to run a spiritual development group and I encouraged her to take this step. She eventually decided she would start a group on the 3rd April. I asked her if it would be okay for me to go and although she felt that I wouldn't learn anything, she said she would be honoured to have me attend.

I went along to the group and all the members were female accept for one person, John, it was really lovely to meet him properly. As there were people who didn't know each other, we all had to introduce ourselves. I told everyone about my work and that I used to run a spiritual shop. As I was talking about the shop, I heard John say "Oh right". He told me later on that he had learned Reiki in my shop and it began to make sense that this was the person I should have met over a decade ago.

The group met at Annie's again on the 8th May, we had a really positive evening and it was good for me to be able to sit and meditate. After we finished I had the opportunity of talking to John about his work. I finally felt ready to do something about my eating problems and I asked John if the EFT would help me. He assured me that it would so I made an appointment to see him on the 21st May.

I was very nervous on the way to John's home. It was my choice to go and see him as I didn't want my partner finding out. He didn't like me talking to men and would have objected if John had come to me. He used to get angry when I did readings for members of the opposite sex, but at that time, most of my clients were female.

John was very kind and explained to me more about the EFT and how it could help. It is like acupuncture without the needles and certain points on the hands and face are lightly tapped, whilst you say statements about how you feel. Quite often the point at which you start is not where you end up, but gradually the root of the problem comes to the surface.

I had gone to John for my weight problems and he started working with me on this. As I was tapping and saying my statements, I suddenly felt a wave of emotion come up. I realised that the reason I had gained weight was to protect myself from my partner. My partner made me feel bad about myself and that I was unworthy and had no confidence or self-belief.

As John worked with the issues of my weight which was the cause of these emotions I suddenly started to get very upset. He kept asking me to go back to times that made me feel these emotions where the negative feelings started. He asked me if any other men had made me feel like this and I suddenly remembered how I was made to feel when I had the termination years earlier.

The man I had been with had not supported me when I got pregnant, he felt that I had done it deliberately and he made me feel so guilty and worthless for what I had done. The termination had made me feel so bad about myself and the feelings of guilt that I had every Valentine's Day still remained.

John was really supportive and helped me so much that day. He continued to help offering support and suggestions of what to tap on.

Through releasing these emotions, something else had started to change and I started to become aware of a man in spirit around me often, but I wasn't sure who it was. He used to link in with me in the most bizarre way and it felt like he was putting a tube up my right nostril. It had started immediately I left John and happened more and more over the next few weeks.

After I left John, I had to return home. My partner was very angry as I had been out for ages and didn't tell him where I had gone. He started to shout at me, as I answered back I saw his fist come towards me. I ducked and ran out of the door telling him I was never going to let him treat me like that again.

He came running after me and tried to get into the car, but I locked it from the inside. He was standing in front of me and I just wanted to run him over, but something stopped me. I finally backed the car away from him and went for a drive to calm down. On my return, his attitude was very different. This was the start of me becoming stronger and I know this was the result of the EFT I had with John.

As part of my EFT for weight loss, I had started to do a strict detox diet. I was allergic to wheat, dairy, yeast and sugar. A friend of mine had told me about the anti-candida diet she had tried and lost 3.1/2 stone. I had considerably more to lose than this, but as I had tried every diet going in the past without success I thought I would give it a try.

It was really strict and I had to cut out all of these foods including fruit, which contains a lot of natural sugar. It seemed quite hard at first, I had to read the ingredients of everything, but I was determined to stick to it.

John had told me about a fair he was running with another clairvoyant and asked if I would like to take part. I agreed to do it and we kept in contact about it. I had a really bad feeling about the event which was due to take place in the July, but I still agreed and tried to help John.

Sadly I was right, John walked away from the event and I didn't take part. I knew this had really knocked his confidence and I had the idea of running another one, with a totally different idea. I asked John if he would be interested in organizing one with me, he said he would love to. So we started to plan the event for the following December. People often get bored around Christmas, so I thought 29th December would be ideal. We planned what we were going to offer and started to spend time organizing it.

We used to meet regularly for coffee to discuss the plans and we started to become really good friends. I had discovered at the group that John had a passion for lemon cake. I used to take cakes along for the group to share. Every so often I would make a cake just for him. He used to say it was the best lemon cake in the world!

The detox diet had made me feel quite ill, and I was in bed with a raging temperature and sore throat. When you eliminate these poisons from your system, your body throws out all the toxins resulting initially in feeling quite ill. I had texted John to say I was feeling really ill and he promised to send me some healing. I am sure it helped as I started to feel much better.

Distance healing is very effective, we are all energy and providing we ask our guides for permission to send healing for the highest good, it is okay to do this as the healing energy just carries through the Universe and is given to the other person.

As I was lying in bed just after receiving John's text about the healing, I felt the gentleman from spirit around me again. I suddenly realised it was John's dad. I texted him again to ask if I could speak to him, as I was sure that it was his dad trying to get a message through.

John had just started a new job and was on call, but he said that he would ring as soon as he could. While I was waiting for the call I started to write down information that his dad told me. When John called me a couple of hours later I told him what I had experienced and gave him the information. He said he would check it out and get back to me.

A couple of days later John texted me to say he could verify all the information. I arranged to pop over and see him the following evening to talk about it.

When I arrived, John told me that everything I had given him was true. We explored the reading in more detail and everything started to make sense. At this point I realised that the gentleman I had been picking up on for ages was indeed John's dad.

It felt quite strange that I suddenly had John's dad around me so often, but I knew that he was there to help us both I used to pick up messages for John and pass them over through email, they were never urgent. But one Saturday morning I felt his dad and I started to get the same old uncomfortable feeling that I had when something was going to happen.

I remembered that John was going to Thorpe Park with his son and I just felt so frightened for them. His dad was saying "be careful on the vampire ride". Normally I would not have contacted John when he had his little boy as I know these times are very special for them both.

I tried to ignore the feelings I was being given, but I couldn't. I knew I had to try and warn him so I sent him a text saying "I have your dad with me and he is telling me you must not go on the vampire ride, something is not right". I knew that John probably wouldn't respond, I just had to trust that he got the message.

I was really surprised to get a message back with the two words "we're safe". I was so relieved but still had this heavy feeling. I responded back to him saying "I'm glad, but I still need to tell you to be careful".

All I could do was visualize John and his son surrounded by a protective light. I knew he was a free spirit and I couldn't prevent him from doing what he wanted, so I just asked his dad to protect them both.

I didn't hear anything else, so I assumed everything was okay. A couple of days later I received an email saying he had got my second message and still decided to use his "free will" and go back on the ride. He said there were no problems on the first ride, but they had decided to go on it again later in the day. This time the ride was unusually bumpy and at one point it stopped very suddenly and then continued at top speed again.

John said shortly after the ride, his son had complained that he felt ill, so the trip was brought to a sudden end and they left early to go home. He went on to say the next day he had woken up with a painful shoulder and back, he realised that it was the jolting on the ride that caused it. He thanked me and said I was right to have contacted him, even though he thought I had lost the plot. So in the grand scheme of things, the warnings I had been given were correct and I was right to follow my intuition to pass the messages on.

Since I met John I really don't know what happened, maybe he activated something within my spiritual development, maybe it was to do with his dad linking with me, but my Mediumship went "bang" after the EFT session. I found that I was linking to more spirit people and my readings started to change as I began to work with this side more.

I would like to explain a little about the Mediumship as not everyone understands what it is about. A Medium is a person who receives messages from people that have passed to spirit. It is said that everyone has a certain ability to do this, but not many people choose to use it as most of the time they don't understand.

Mental Mediumship is separated into different ways of working.

Clairvoyance (clear seeing) is when the Medium sees the spirit person and is able to give a detailed description through the third eye. Some can even see spirit with the physical eyes, just as if they were in the room.

Clairaudience (clear hearing) is when the actual voice is heard, but for some the voices are heard in their mind.

Clairsentience (clear sensing) is probably the most common style used to day. The Mediums senses spirit near them. They can sense sex, build, height, physical appearance, illnesses, character and conditions of passing. Through this they are able to pass on any words they wish to give to the sitter.

Claircognizance (clear knowing). This is where the Medium just "knows" something to be correct, but they are unable to substantiate this with fact, or how they get that particular information. An example is when you finish off a sentence for someone else, before they have finished. Many people can do this, they just don't realise they are picking up on something spiritual.

I work with all four of these senses and sometimes hear the information clearly, other times it may be a picture or a symbol I am given. The way in which I work is down to the person communicating from the other side. When we return to spirit, we have to learn how to communicate with those on the earth plane, in the same way that a Medium has to learn how to contact spirit. It is a bit like learning lessons at school.

One of the questions I am asked most is, "do spirit have to leave a certain amount of time before they can contact us?" Although many Mediums say six months, I have had people through the day after they have passed.

One of my friends called Anne, lost her mum with cancer. I was able to tell Anne that her funeral should be simple; she wanted her family to enjoy her hard earned cash, not the undertaker. Anne's husband had been discussing this with her, as he felt that she should be given a proper funeral out of respect. But Anne knew her mum wouldn't have wanted the fuss. So Anne was able to respect her mum's wishes. The following is taken from a letter that Anne has written to me, she wants to tell you her story:

I've known Sally for many years now and remembering the first time I met her, it was her passion and knowledge in all things Pagan/Wiccan, that consolidated many thoughts that were already setting the seeds of my own belief system and inspired me to explore more. I watched Sally as her spiritual pathway developed, grew stronger and her confidence increased to become the person she now is.

I'm not one of Sally's closest friends but occasionally, she'll ring me, 'You've been on my mind – what's the matter?" And sure enough I would have something going on. I've had several readings with her, and of course it could have been easy, should I have ever to have doubted her integrity and professionalism, to tell me what I wanted to hear...... she never has done that, and I have never had reason to doubt what she tells me.

There are certain things she's told me she just could not have known, on the earthly plane, but on the spirit planes – oh yes!

My Mum died in 2007, I had a reading a few days after she died. Sally had rung; Mum had been trying to attract Sally's attention. I was a bit skeptical 'spirits don't come through this quick!' Sally listened to spirit and Mum told her my Dad's name – never discussed that with Sally, I always called him Dad and the newspaper announcement had not yet been published. Mum said she didn't approve of young children being at funerals. That was so 'Mum'! She also emphasized the significance of pink and purple flowers. We ordered pink and purple flowers for the funeral. This bemused my Dad a bit as he'd not ever realised pink and purple flowers were her favourite, actually neither had I, she liked all flowers! A few days after Mum's funeral it was my birthday, my Dad handed me an envelope containing my birthday card, I opened it to discover a simple card adorned with colourful pink & purple flowers, the last card Mum chose before she died and for that reason Dad had signed it form Dad & Mum. I knew then that's what my Mum meant – it was us that didn't understand.

In 2009 I planned a solo trip to India, Nepal and Thailand, an important trip for me, of self-discovery and testing comfort zones. A reading with Sally prior to the journey revealed I was to meet a man, who would become a very important part of my life. The excitement of anticipation building - a lover? No – it's not a romantic liaison, possibly a past life connection. 'His name is G.. Ger.. Ga...' struggled Sally ' I can't get his name, something like Gaspa? Oh I really don't understand what they're saying, I can't say it'.

Slightly disappointed, how can you travel to exotic places and meet a man, I'd decided a French man probably called Jasper or Gaspard? How on earth would he be important in my life?

The reading totally forgotten, I immersed myself in joys and despairs of travelling and at this time, teaching English in a Tibetan Buddhist Monastery in Nepal. Three of us lived there and taught English to the novice monks, the greatest bunch of guys you could ever hope to meet. We developed our own system of descriptive nicknames for several of them e.g. Glasses Guy & 'The older one, who always talks to me'. All the lads loved to practice speaking English and we spent lots of time outside classes talking. 'The older one' an 18yr old, wasn't in our classes. During term time he was at college in India but the monastery was his home during his vacation. His English was good, his vocabulary was huge and he spent a lot of time with me, talking to me, explaining many points of Buddhist philosophy. If I was there - he would appear. One morning, I sat on the steps alone, writing my diary. My entry was to be a report of an amazing conversation I'd had the previous evening with 'The older one'. To this day that entry still just says 'Amazingly' because at that point he appeared and sat beside me and started talking. I decided to ask his name and he wrote it in my diary because it was one I'd not heard before.

His name is Gyatso.

He continues to communicate regularly, he tells me of his progress on his nine year Buddhist Philosophy course and college life. I returned last year and he unexpectedly 'adopted' me as his Mom. His own mother died when he was 5 and he put in the Monastery at the age of 6.

And yes - Gyatso is an important part in my life!

Amazing readings Sally – just rubbish at pronouncing foreign names!   I'll forgive you though………

From Anne - May 2011

Another friend Karen lost her dear papa. He was concerned that his wife would have very expensive flowers at the funeral as a tribute to him. He asked for a simple bunch of purple Iris. Karen's mum still insisted on something a little more than a bunch of Iris, but the Iris flowers were put into a lavish wreath. To this day, whenever Karen's dad comes through he always mentions the expensive flowers.

When we lose our loved ones, we want them to have the best possible send off, but they are around us and don't need lavish funerals. Money is for the physical world, not something that is part of spirit, but we must always honour what we feel is the right thing to do.

A New Home

My home life was becoming so difficult and I prayed for help and guidance every day. I had started to lose weight really quickly, as the pounds fell off; I became mentally stronger and physically fitter. My confidence had grown to an all-time high and I was ready to take the next important step in my life.

I had asked my partner to leave on numerous occasions, but he said he was not going to be forced out of "his home". I really didn't know where I was going to find somewhere to live, I had no money and my credit history was really bad. Although I had sold the shop, I was struggling to pay off the debts that had accumulated.

I had been insured for sickness to cover loans for stock and the hefty overdraft, but when I tried to make a claim to cover this, the bank refused to help me, saying they could not pay out on an existing illness.

One morning I woke up to find my partner in a particularly foul mood. I knew that I couldn't continue my life in this way, my spiritual pathway was so important and he did everything he could to stop me.

My friend Elaine had come round to visit me that particular day, my partner didn't like Elaine, and she was a very strong and would stick up for herself. I had been friends with Elaine for many years, way before we both started our different spiritual pathways. Elaine was the one who introduced me to my experience of past life regression and she had also told me about Holman House in Aylsham, where I should have gone for the psychic supper years earlier. Elaine was the only person who knew the trauma I went through and she was very understanding, always trying to give me ways to move on.

When my partner left, I broke down into floods of tears and told Elaine I couldn't go on anymore. She said to me "perhaps you are looking at it from the wrong angle. Maybe you should walk away and tell him he can have the house". Something changed within me at that moment and I realised I didn't want the house anyway. It was full of bad memories that I would never be able to forget in a million years. I knew that my partner was so very materialistic and I felt that I could finally do something about the situation.

I made my decision and started to look for somewhere to rent. because of my credit history, none of the letting agencies would take me on. I managed to find a company that would and they told me there was a bungalow that was for rent. The monthly rental fee was £850 per month and I needed to put the same down again as a deposit. It was very expensive, but I knew that if I worked really hard, I would be able to scrape by each month. I knew that spirit would always look after me, that much I trusted.

I went back and told my partner I was leaving him, I told him he could have the house but I wanted the money for the deposit and rent on the bungalow. I also told him I wanted a further £6,000. Our house was worth £169,000, the prices of property had soared since we purchased, so there was about £100,000 equity in it. The sum I asked for was a mere pittance in comparison to what he would gain.

He told me that he didn't have any money, which I knew was a lie. His antiques business was bringing in so much money and I knew he wasn't short. I told him that I needed to have the money so I could move out and that he could pay the rest later. He agreed he would give me £1,800 but I had to sign an agreement to say that I would not make any further claims on the property. I would have signed my life away, if I thought I could have my freedom, so I agreed and it was sorted out.

I contacted the agency and they told me the property wasn't available until the 8th October. I had arranged with a friend to look after her cat whilst she went on holiday, so I knew that I didn't have long to wait.

I moved into my friend's house and it was heaven. I was able to continue my readings from there and everything was okay. I knew that I could move straight into the bungalow when she returned from her holiday, so I was happy with the fact that I never needed to live with him again.

A few weeks before I moved out, my partner had read my emails and discovered I was doing an event with John. He became very angry and made my life a misery. Because of this, most of the discussions were through email. I was occasionally able to escape to meet John for a coffee, but when I stayed at my friend's house we talked on the phone every night to discuss the event.

The two weeks I was at my friend's house flew by and the relief of knowing I had not got to go back really inspired me that things were finally falling into place.

The bungalow was perfect for what I needed, it had a lovely big conservatory and I planned to run development groups and workshops from there.

October 31st was Halloween and I had been invited to celebrate the pagan festival of Samhain with the other members of the pagan group. I decided I wanted to dress up as a witch, but I didn't want to be an ordinary witch. I scoured the internet to find a costume and found a lovely sexy witch outfit. I had lost several stone by this time and as I put the short dress on, I felt so good.

When I arrived, my friends were amazed at how good I looked. There were several people I hadn't seen for a while; some of them hadn't recognised me. This gave me a real sense of achievement.

John came to join the celebrations and we were chatting and mixing with everyone. Suddenly I had a really strange feeling and I looked across the room and saw John looking at me. As I returned the gaze, our eyes became locked together, everyone in the room disappeared. I don't know what was going through his mind, or mine, but it brought up some really lovely feelings for me. We held each other's gaze for what felt like ages, but something special had happened. I will never forget that moment as long as I live, it was almost as if our minds were locked together.

Looking back I feel it was probably a soul connection. I had always believed that John and I had been together in many past lives. I know at that time he didn't really believe in past life connections, but I know he is more open to this now.

My contact with John's dad continued and he asked me to take his son to the beach on the full moon for healing. I asked John if he would like to do this and he said he was up for anything.

The full moon was on the 13th November, so we drove to Mundesley, where he had been born. It was very misty and although we couldn't see the moon, the sky was bright and the beach was warm and sheltered from the wind. After we had completed the healing ceremony, I gave John a single yellow rose to place in the sea in memory of his dad. I placed a rose for my Gran and a further rose to signify our friendship.

I was so taken aback by the gentleness of this man as he bent down and gently placed the rose into the sea. It is a very different side to the one that he normally shows people. As John bent down, I suddenly had a vision of him being swept out to sea and I wanted to hold onto his arm, just in case he left me.

Placing the roses in the sea was to be more significant than we ever knew and would link us to one of my future clients.

Just after the evening on the beach, I suddenly thought that I would like to do some public demonstrations, something I had said I would never do, but my guides had other plans for me.

A few days later I received a call from a lady saying she was going to start doing demonstrations and asked if I would like to do one for her the following February. I agreed and then started to panic, what if I couldn't do it and made a fool of myself? But I trusted that the spirit world knew I was ready to work in this way. Two days after I had agreed to do the demonstration, I received a call from a landlady asking if I would do a charity evening in her public house. The evening was booked for the week after the first event.

I figured that if I wasn't ready, spirit would not have given me this opportunity as well. I trust spirit with my life and I know they will never let me down.

The event with John was going smoothly and we had planned to have presentations throughout the day. I asked him if I could do some Mediumship and he was going to a presentation on his own work.

The panic started to set in and I realised that if I was putting myself in the public arena, I ought to get some practise. So I started to arrange a few evenings at my home. The conservatory was big enough to seat about 16, so I did a few evenings leading up to the event.

I was still following my really strict eating plan and the weight was falling off so quickly and I was dropping a dress size every few weeks. The only problem with this was that I didn't have much money to spare to replace my baggy clothes. I lived in cheap tops and jeans but I realised that I was soon going to have to start buying smart clothes to work in.

It was really good standing in front of the mirror and seeing the new slim me, I had become the incredible shrinking woman.

I remembered that night I had done the healing on the beach with John, it had a profound effect on me. I felt a really strong link to this man who was responsible for me having the courage to make the decision to move on with my life in a positive way. I will always be grateful for this amazing man.

Christmas was looming and I was busy with preparations for the fair, I busied myself working out the last details for the event. My ex-partner had told me he was taking our daughter away for Christmas. I was really upset, but I didn't want him to think that I was going to come between their relationship, so I let her go.

On Christmas Eve, my daughter went off with her dad and I busied myself with the last details of the event. It seemed very strange without her, but I had the boys with me. I knew my middle son was going back to his girlfriends after Christmas lunch, but my eldest was spending the rest of the day and evening with me.

I had refused an invitation to go to a friend's house for the evening, as I didn't want to leave him on his own. After Christmas lunch, Adam announced he was going to go and stay with his friend, so I was left on my own.

It seemed very strange being on my own on Christmas Day. I had been surrounded by people for years and I had to come to terms with the loneliness. I knew I had made the right decision, but these feelings of being alone in the world were hard to cope with.

I kept myself busy for the rest of the day but the loneliness kept coming back. I was really grateful that John had agreed to do the event with me as it gave me something to do.

I was relieved that Christmas was over and the next couple of days went really quickly. I decided I needed to go and buy something to wear for our event. By this time I had lost even more weight and was down to a size 14. I went into Jane Norman and found the most perfect dress. It was grey and purple and cut with a flattering empire line. It was a little low at the neck and I put a stitch in as I felt a little self-conscious as the dress was shorter than I had worn for many years and I didn't want to break the fashion rules of mixing a low neckline with a short dress.

The morning of the event arrived and I put my dress on. I felt like a million dollars and was hoping John would notice my new slim figure. I had arranged to meet him at 7.30am to put the tables out. I knew John had got his son with him but he said he would still be there on time. One thing I have learned is that my friend is very rarely on time for anything. By the time John finally arrived, my daughter and I had got everything in place; Despite my efforts to look good, I don't think John would have noticed if I had been wearing a bin bag. John said he had to take his son back to his mum and said he would be about an hour and a half.

The stallholders arrived and although there were a few hiccups, everything got sorted out. Later that morning, things started to go wrong. The heater stopped working and people were complaining it was cold. I was doing readings at the time and went to look for John to sort it out. He was nowhere to be found, but I eventually settled everyone down again.

I was a bit concerned that John had seemed to have vanished, so I went outside to look for him. He came walking round the corner without a care in the world and I was so cross that he had left me to sort things out on my own. I asked him why he hadn't been there to give me the help I needed and he just replied "well I'm here now". John seemed very subdued, I had never seen him like this before so I asked him what was wrong, and he just said "nothing".

At this point a friend of mine arrived, Sara was a reporter and I asked her if she would talk to John about his work they disappeared into the other room and John started to cheer up.

I realised that it was almost time to do my demonstration, I was so nervous. I went into the room where Sara and John sat and suddenly people started to come in and sit down.

I started to sense spirit around me and gave messages from their loved ones. At one point John looked up and realised that people were standing, so he went off to find more chairs.

The last message I received was from a young man who had taken an overdose. I felt a sickness in my mouth and stomach it was almost as I felt that I was choking. I realised I had picked up on the last few moments of this young man.

The message he gave was so profound, he told me that he had been very depressed and had been planning his death for a few weeks. He waited for the family to go away on holiday and then he took the tablets. He wanted me to say that he was sorry for the pain he had put him family through, but they were powerless to help him and the depression he had sunk into.

He asked me to pass on the following message to everyone and the words will stay with me forever. He said "Never be afraid of telling the people you love, that you love them. Never be afraid to say sorry to the people you have hurt. Don't wait until you pass to the spirit world to say these words, because I have waited patiently to be able to express these words to my family".

The words meant so much and it had a profound effect on my life and work. I make a really big effort to follow his advice, and I always share my true feelings with people even if they don't want to hear it. Sometimes people find it hard to accept the words "I love you", but I feel we should say them anyway.

I have been able to forgive everyone in my life who has caused me pain and misery. I always say sorry if I feel I have upset someone with my words. We all make mistakes, the secret is to admit them and move on. None of us are perfect, we are all equal. We come into the world with nothing and we leave with nothing.

It was really lovely working with John, even though we had a few things go wrong on the day, but that is to be expected when you are putting on an important event. The event we had organized together made us both realise that we have to be honest with each other. John admitted later that he should have not taken on his full time job as it took up so much time and he felt he couldn't put the effort in that he felt he should. Big lessons were learned by both of us and we both appreciated each other's frustrations a bit more.

In the New Year, I decided to start a development group again. Now that I had the space, I was able to run it from home. There were about twenty people in the group and it is a lovely way to learn and be able to practise your abilities. Some of the group became friends and in particular, one of them has been a great support to me, to this day.

Paula had been a tarot reader for many years, but she came along to see what it was all about. Paula has a wicked sense of humour and I took to her straight away. Paula is a terrific person to be around and her energy is grounded. She works in a slightly different way to me, but she is very accurate in her readings.

Paula was one of the people I gave a message to when I was teaching the group about Mediumship. I gave her several names, that she didn't know, but the next time she came to group, she told me that she had found out about her relatives and was able to clarify everything.

January was a busy month, I was not only doing personal readings but went out and did ladies evenings for small groups of them doing mini readings. I loved working with people and life seemed to have taken a different direction.

The Yellow Rose and Purple Tulips

I met a lady called Lisa just after Christmas. She was really upset and confused when I started to work with her. I could sense that her brother was in spirit and was very upset with what had gone on after he had left the earth plane.

There seemed to be a lot of legal things going on and Lisa was on the point of giving up. Her brother was insistent that she should not. He brother told me that his ashes had still not been scattered, even though many years had elapsed since his passing. Lisa said that she didn't want to scatter the ashes until the legal things were resolved, but I told her that her brother felt she should do this now.

She told me the details of what had happened with her brother. At the time of his passing he had been divorced for a number of years. When the solicitor was sorting out the will, it came to light that the final divorce papers had not been signed, the paperwork done by the original solicitor had forgotten to do it. Technically he was still married and the divorce was not legal.

When his ex-wife found out, she put a claim in for his property and money that Peter had left to his family, claiming that she was the next of kin. Peter had no children, so she had a valid claim.

I told Lisa that she still needed to scatter the ashes, as Peter wanted to be laid to rest. Lisa said she did not know where to scatter the ashes, but her brother had asked me to tell Lisa to go to the place where he felt most at peace when he was here. This was the seaside, where he spent a lot his time.

I told Lisa that her brother had asked me to give her a single yellow rose. She told me that she was not sure what this meant, but I told her it would make sense eventually.

A few days later I received a message from Lisa, saying that she went to Mundesley beach to scatter Peter's ashes. As she was watching the waves taking out the ashes, a single yellow rose came back on the crest of the wave.

When I got the message from Lisa telling me about the yellow rose, I thought about the yellow roses that John and I had placed in the sea a few months earlier.

I am sure that the rose that Lisa got back, was unconnected, but it is something that I have always wondered about. As we know, there are many strange things that happen when spirit is involved.

I think that is rather strange that although I do so many readings, there are some that stay in my memory bank and Lisa's one of those that I will always remember.

I stated earlier in my book I am a firm believer that physical disease can come from unresolved emotions. Just after I left my partner, I was diagnosed with Cervical Cancer; I was totally distraught by the news as my life was happy for the first time in years. I didn't know what to do, so I emailed John to ask for his help.

I knew EFT would be able to shift it, but was unsure what my body was telling me. John emailed me to explain that he felt the reason it had happened was because it was a part of my body that had not been nourished. He gave me suggestions on what to tap on and the statements I needed to work with. I took on board his suggestions and I received the all clear from the doctors a few weeks later.

Fluke or miracle, I don't know, but a reminder that I could self-heal with positive thought and releasing my pent up emotions.

I was still losing weight and it continued to drop off quickly. I decided that I needed to do some exercise to tone up my body a little more. I had started a Fusion Belly Dancing Class a few months previously and I really enjoyed the mixture of Salsa moves and Belly Dancing. My birth sign is Aries, but unlike the typical Arians who are supposed to be athletic, I am not. So I decided to join another dance class, this time Salsa which is a good way of keeping the body toned and having a lot of fun at the same time.

My life was so busy with work and dancing, there was not much time left for anything else, but I liked it that way. I have never been one for sitting around waiting for something to happen. My relationship had made me very reclusive, so I spent as much time as I could with other people. Working from home meant that I did not have to leave my daughter and I arranged my ladies nights and dance classes to coincide with her staying with her dad. I still had my sons living with me, but with their girlfriends the house was never empty!

I had been asked to attend a spiritual evening by a friend Maura and she asked me if I would give a demonstration of belly dancing. John was also asked if he would come along and do a presentation about his EFT. Maura was the kind of person you couldn't say "no" too so I reluctantly formed a circle with everyone and showed them a few basic steps, most people joined, including John.

A few days early John and I had a slight disagreement, as friends do, I wasn't sure if he would turn up. But I guess it was spirits way of getting us to sort things out. It is not very spiritual to leave disagreements unresolved, but we are both stubborn. I was really pleased to see him; we had fallen out over something really silly and I felt so bad.

After his presentation, I broke the ice by complimenting him on his talk. I commented that he was so much more confident than the first one he had done and reminded him how nervous he was the very first time I met him. John had to leave early, but we gave each other a big hug before he left and I felt so much better. I have never been one to hold grudges and it hurt me to think I wouldn't see him again. But it was resolved and our friendship was able to continue.

Maura had given John some tulip bulbs, which he had forgotten, so she asked me if I could take them home for him. Although I wasn't sure if I was going to see him again, I took them anyway; I thought I could always put them in the post. A few days later, I got an email from John complimenting me on the belly dancing. He asked me what had happened to his Tulips, they had been given to him as he was the best male belly dancer. I emailed him and said that I had got them and would he like me to post them. He said he would come and collect them. I knew then that he had forgiven me and me him for our cross words.

A few days later he called round to collect them, but as he was going out the door without the tulips, I put them in his hands and he asked me to plant them and look after them, but he would be keeping an eye on them to make sure I was nurturing them.

The evening was looming even closer for my first public demonstration; unlike the one I had done at the fair with John it was to be the first one as a professional stage medium.

When I had been booked to do the evening, I was told I would be working with another Medium. I was doubly nervous as I had found out that the other person was the one John had walked away from doing an event with. I have said about how spiritual people are not always nice, so I was a bit concerned as she had put the blame on me for John walking away. I always think spirit work in the most amazing ways, so perhaps we had been placed together to sort it out.

As I have said before, I don't blame anyone for their behavior, I tend to forgive and forget, but it was evident in her attitude whilst I was working that she had a problem with me. Little did I know that spirit would be putting us together several times in the future until we did sort it out.

I thoroughly enjoyed the evening and spirit didn't let me down. I had some lovely messages and evidence to pass on. I finished each reading by giving the person I was working with a single rose from their loved ones.

As I had got ready for my evening, I looked in the mirror and the image that reflected back was half the woman I used to be. With the help of the EFT I had lost an amazing 9.1/2 stone since starting my new healthy eating plan. I used to laugh at my friends by saying "I used to be an extra-large, now I 'm a Medium".

Losing the weight changed my whole world. My new regime was very strict and I had to give up wheat, dairy, yeast and sugar. These were all things that my body was allergic to and as soon as I realised this, the weight started to drop off. I had done every possible diet imaginable, but to be honest I never lost a thing. I can remember joining a local slimming club and following the diet to the letter, only to gain weight. They thought I had cheated, but I know now it was because their diet was made up of a lot of carbohydrates and unfortunately the bread and cereal made me gain weight.

As a result of the weight loss, my health improved and I had so much energy. My dress size had dropped from a 22 to a 14 and it was fantastic to be able to pick up anything off the rails and know it would fit me.

I am truly grateful for the help John gave me helping me to release the emotions that had kept my weight on. I believe that extra weight is caused because we are trying to protect ourselves. Obviously over eating causes the weight gain as we do tend to either overeat or lose weight, whichever our weakness is. The old adage of fat people being happy certainly doesn't resonate with me. I was totally embarrassed and miserable.

My first demonstration gave me a taste of what it was like to be in the public eye. I really loved it and although I enjoyed all of my work, the demonstrations allow me to reach even more people.

I will always remember my second demonstration; I had been booked to do a charity evening in a Public House. I was told that they were going to close the public bar and I was to work in a large bar at the back of the pub. When I arrived, there were about 70 people watching. I had taken another Medium with me, who wanted to gain some confidence, I sometimes give others the opportunity to work in this way, but not everyone is cut out for this way of working.

I started the evening off and the other Medium went second. As she finished her message the sound equipment started buzzing and there was a lot of noise in the front of the pub. Unfortunately the bar had been left open in the room we were working in and the audience were getting up and buying drinks. This is very distracting and I always insist on a bar being closed whilst I am working now. At this point, we decided to have a short break. The other Medium decided she didn't want to work anymore, so I knew that I would be working for the entire second half. I am used to working on my own, so I really didn't have a problem with it.

As I started back I had the sense of a young man who had passed to spirit recently linking in with me. He made me aware that he had taken his own life. I described him as a slim and fit looking man, around the age of 18. I made my link to a member of the audience and continued the message. I sensed he had multiple injuries, which seemed to be inconsistent with the way people normally take their own life. As I was talking to my recipient, I became aware of a lady sobbing. I knew it was his

Mum and I asked if she was okay talking to me. Although she was extremely upset, she said she was okay for me to continue. I gave her a lot of personal details about her son, but most importantly the message was that she should not blame herself, no one could have prevented him from doing what he did. He was very sorry for the devastation he had left behind; he knew his family blamed themselves. As I was working with this lovely young man, he showed me a railway track and I asked his mum if it made any sense. She confirmed that it did.

The evening went well and I was able to place all the lovely spirit messages to their connections here. When I worked in the early days, I wasn't always sure who I was linking with, but now I get a beautiful light around the person.

After the demonstration, the young man's mum came up to talk to me. She told me that her son had thrown himself off a railway bridge under an oncoming train two weeks previously. The noise that we heard from the front of the pub was because her son's friends had come in drinking to celebrate his wake as the funeral had taken place earlier that day.

I think this lady showed amazing courage; she had just buried her son but had come to a public demonstration. I don't think there are many people who could have done that. I was honoured to be able to give her a message from him and I hoped that she realised there was nothing she could do to help the depression he had suffered from.

It is very amazing to me the evidence that spirit are able to give me. I feel my role is as an Ambassador for the spirit world and I feel very privileged to be able to work in this way.

From the demonstrations, I often get groups of people ask me to do readings for them, so I returned to the area to give readings for several ladies. The hostess was the last person I did a reading for and I picked up that she had been in a terribly violent relationship, which she confirmed to be was true. I was also able to tell her that her cousin had helped her to get out of the marriage.

The information I was given had come from her cousin who was spirit side. He had taken his own life a few years previously. A few months before he died, he had bought a house. The property was really old and it had a very high wooden beam running across the living room. Her cousin had bought the house and chosen it for the beam, always intending to take his own life. He had a very tragic life himself and had lost both his parents many years previously. His marriage had ended and felt he couldn't go on anymore.

The last time he saw his cousin, he promised her that he would do something to help her get out of the violent marriage she was in. A few weeks later, he was found hanging from the beam. He told me that he had searched to find a house that would allow him to carry out his suicide, but he wanted to help his cousin so that his death wasn't in vain.

After the reading, she told me that her cousin had left her the house and all his money. It meant that she was able to buy another property and leave her violent marriage. It is ironical that even though her cousin chose to end in such a sad way, he was able to help someone else through his own death.

When I first realised I wanted to work in the public eye, I felt that I needed to work on my stage presentation. I had heard about it a place at Stanstead called The Arthur Findley College of Psychic Development. This is a teaching Centre that people come to from all over the world to learn about healing and developing their psychic skills. I checked the website and found they did all types of courses. A course that I was drawn to was called "Stand Up For Spirit". It was for people wanting to work on their connection to the spirit world and their stage presentation. The course was being run by Tony Stockwell, one of the world's most famous Mediums

On Saturday 4th April 2008, I got in the car to drive to Stanstead. It was the first time I had ever driven that far on my own. Although I had been driving for over 25 years, my journeys were always local. I was so nervous about getting there that John came to the rescue once more and lent me his "Road Angel" sat nav. I knew with a name like that would get there safely. It was about a two hour journey and I left in plenty of time allowing myself a break in the middle. It was the first time in my life I had ever done something for myself and on my own.

As I was driving, I was questioning my ability, would I be good enough? How would I get on not knowing anyone? Would my confidence let me down? All of these thoughts and hundreds more were going through my mind. I almost turned round and went home, but I knew despite my fears I had to go. I arrived on time, with only one detour. I had ended up in the Airport car park.

I checked in at reception and was told to join the queue as Tony Stockwell was interviewing everyone personally to see which group they would be in. As I went into the main hall way there was a large queue of people in front of me. I saw Tony sitting there chatting and smiling and my heart missed a beat, a thousand butterflies in my tummy. I had never been so close to someone this famous before!

I had seen Tony in a demonstration at the Theatre Royal in Norwich a couple of years before, I never dreamed that I would see him this close up, let alone talk to him.

I took my place and waited for an hour until it was my turn. As I sat down opposite Tony he smiled and his beautiful blue eyes shone brightly. Tony asked me if I had done any public demonstrations or readings and asked me why I wanted to do the course. I replied that I had been doing readings for several years and had done a few public demonstrations. I told him that I wanted a better connection to spirit so that I could help people get the proof they needed that there is no such thing as physical death, merely a shedding of the physical body, spirit lives on eternally.

Tony was a lovely gentle soul and his natural sense of humour put me at my ease. He told me that he would decide which group to place me in and it would be put on the board in the hall by the next morning.

I left Tony and went to find my room and the people I would be sharing with. Stanstead Hall is a beautiful old building. The energy was lovely and calming with a peaceful atmosphere. It is set in well maintained grounds that have a natural beauty and vibrancy. I felt like I had come home.

My course was a week long, but I had a sense of belonging in that atmosphere. I knew I would enjoy my time there. I was lucky to have two lovely roommates, who made me feel very welcome. They had both done the course before.

As I have described, the building was very old and I was surprised to find that there were old fashioned baths that seemed to take forever to fill. But that didn't really matter; I have always been an early riser, so I managed to get to the bathroom before anyone else in the mornings.

Before I had left for Stanstead, I had a reading with someone and they told me to look out for a man wearing a ring with a blue stone in it. As I went to the dining room for dinner that evening, we were told that we were to sit in the same place each mealtime for the duration of our stay. The dining room was quite full and I managed to find a space to sit with five other people. As we began introducing ourselves, I noticed the man opposite me was wearing a ring with a blue stone! I thought this was a pretty amazing piece of confirmation. Although I had been told about this, I didn't believe it would happen, nor did I find out what the significance was.

We were given a programme of the week ahead, it was quite intense and full, we had little free time and even the evenings were taken up with demonstrations and workshops. After dinner we joined Tony in the Sanctuary and he welcomed us all and told us about the week ahead. He said some of the students would be asked to do demonstrations of Mediumship in front of the teachers and students. We were told to meet in the Sanctuary the next morning after breakfast.

It was a little strange being with so many like-minded people, but as I said, it felt like I had come home. There were people from all over the world, USA, Germany, Ireland and all over the UK.

I got up the next morning and raced down to breakfast; looking on the way to see whose group I had been put in. I was really pleased to find that I had been placed with Tony himself. A couple of the people I shared my dining table with were also in his group, so I didn't feel quite so alone.

After breakfast we all met in the Sanctuary and started the day off with a meditation and inspirational words from Tony and the other teachers. This was to set the ambiance for the day ahead.

I made my way to Tony's room and took my place. We had all been given name badges and I was known as Sally T. This is the name that Tony called me for the duration of the course.

There were over a hundred people on the course and I didn't know anyone. My friend Sara had told me that her friend Marcus was going to be there and told me to look out for him. I didn't know what he looked like, but was sure we would meet up. A couple of days later I literally bumped into a blonde haired man. I didn't take too much notice as I hurried for my next course.

After dinner, the same man was walking towards me; there was some sort of recognition from both of us. At the same time he said "are you Sara's friend Sally?" I said "are you Sara's friend Marcus?" Neither of us had name badges on but somehow we recognised each other. I found Marcus had missed the first couple of days due to work, so there was no way he knew who I was. I always think that synchronicity is a wonderful thing. It is almost as though spirit arranges these meetings at the right time.

I really enjoyed being in Tony's group, he has a good sense of humour but he also pushes you to get the best out of you. Each lesson Tony would get us doing something different so I learned a lot. At the end of the first lesson, Tony called a list of names of people who would be doing demonstrations on the Monday evening, I nearly jumped out of my seat as he said "Sally T you will be demonstrating in the Sanctuary". Everyone knew that the Sanctuary was the biggest place to work in, even though there were several smaller rooms to work in. I also felt very nervous because Tony always sat in on the demonstrations in there and gave feedback with another Tutor.

I couldn't believe that I had been picked to work in front of such a famous and experienced person, I had butterflies just thinking about it.

Tony explained there would be six of us working and we would be required to give a message for about twenty minutes each. He said that along with the other Tutor, he would give us honest feedback. Tony always referred to this as "Critique".

I took my place on the stage and I was the third person to work, I was pleased I wasn't going to be the first And I felt even better that I wasn't going to be the last. I don't think my nerves would have stood that.

I had been told by a friend to wear a red dress, so I was feeling good. I was so pleased with my appearance and I wanted to look professional. As I was sitting waiting for my turn, I was so nervous. One of the students said to me "Do you normally wear fishnet stockings for dems?" I nearly fell off my seat with embarrassment, but I must say they have become a bit of a trademark now and have caused me to be frowned upon in local churches!

Soon it was my turn to get up and do my presentation. There were about a hundred people in the room plus Tony and the other Tutor. The worst thing was that everyone else in the room had the same ability, so it wasn't like a public demonstration where some people did not know how you were working, or what would be given as evidence.

I was deadly nervous as I introduced myself; I then said "Just give me a moment whilst I wait for spirit to arrive as they do". As I stood nervously waiting, I started to sense a gentleman around me. He started to give me his condition of passing and I felt he was in an accident and that he was an older man. I described his build and his clothing. I also got some names given to me. I asked if anyone understood the information and a rather excited voice in a lovely Irish accent shouted out from the back "You are with me!"

I was so pleased to make my link, I was dreading that no one would take it, but I continued on with the message and evidence I had been given. I was also able to describe his injuries. I was given a silver sixpence in my hand. My gentleman told me it was his Grandad and that he used to place a three penny piece in his hand when he was a boy and tell him it was a sixpence. I gave him loads more evidence that he verified. I was so relieved to finish my message.

When I had completed my demonstration, the Tutor started to critique me. She picked up on my opening phrase of "waiting for spirit to arrive" and said she expected them to arrive on a jumbo jet; this caused much hilarity with the other students. She gave me a couple of other things to take on board, which were helpful.

Then it was Tony's turn. He said that I had a "raw ability" that could be worked with. He complimented me on my stage presence, appearance and was really pleased with me for picking up the evidence about the sixpence. He also said he would have liked me to work a bit harder with some of the evidence, but overall, I had done well.

I sat down, relieved it was all over. After the evening had finished, the crowd was dispersing. My lovely Irish man came running down the hall, nearly knocking people over to get to me. He picked me up, twizzled me round and said "I'm going to tell

Tony Stockwell you are the best ******* Medium I have ever seen". He told me I had given him some amazing evidence about his Grandad and his family. His Grandad apparently died in the accident and lost the left side of his body, which was the pain that I was picking up. He took me off to the bar and insisted on buying me a drink.

All of the students headed to the bar after the evenings had finished. It was great to socialize and talk about the events of the day and also to get to know the other groups. Usually the evenings finished off with Irish Dancing as we had some fantastic Irish students there.

The next day was very long and we had to spend time with other Tutors in order to learn different ways of working, as it is a very individual thing. The day ended with Tutor demonstrations and we finished up congregating in the bar once more.

People started to come up to me and congratulate me on the demonstration; apparently I had been much talked about! I got a real buzz thinking people were talking about me in a positive way, I had put up with years of being told I was useless by my ex-partner. This did my confidence the power of good and I felt elated.

It is easy to get carried away with ego and I see so many people working with theirs. But I believe that there should be no ego with our work, we are here to give evidence by communicating with spirit. I hear people blowing their own trumpet all the time in this field about how good they are. This is so unnecessary and Gordon Smith is an advocate of this. The proof I get that I am doing my work properly is when people tell me how happy they are that they have had a message.

My week at Stanstead really helped me, I learned about working with double links – two spirit people working with one Medium, working with two different spirits with two different connections and working with two clients at the same time, one on a psychic link and the other on a Mediumship link. I was taught how to ask for specific details from spirit, i.e. their favourite food or drink and so much more.

I will never forget the help and guidance that Tony gave me in his appraisal at the end of the course. Tony gives you an opinion of your strengths and what you need to do to help yourself. His words will stay in my mind as long as I live. Tony said "I have seen you working all week, you have given some good evidence, and everything I have asked you to do you have taken on board. You have been supportive to your peers and worked well in groups and on your own. I would like to see you doing at least two public demonstrations a week and I feel that within 18months you will really fly. I also see you working on stage with a slightly younger man". I was really pleased with Tony's appraisal and I had confirmation that I was indeed on the right pathway. Strange thing is the man I ended up working with a bit later on was Marcus, the gentleman from the course. Marcus lives miles away, but he comes to Norfolk to work sometimes and we do work well together and have a good laugh as well.

A Prayer to Save My Soul!

When I came back from Stanstead, I found that once again my Mediumship had taken a step up to another level. I knew I had to start to look at arranging more public demonstrations as Tony suggested, so I started to manifest the right person to work with me.

I attended a Mind, Body and Spirit Fair and bumped into my ex business partner. Tracy told me she had started arranging demonstrations for Mediums living in another area. I told her I needed to arrange some for myself, but Tracy said she would be happy to arrange them but she wanted to see me work first, to see what I was capable of doing. I arranged another evening at my home and Tracy was very impressed. The evening went well and Tracy went to find some local venues.

One of the first ones we did was in Tracy's village hall. We were both nervous wondering if anyone would turn up. About ten minutes before I was due to start, a queue started to form. We had over 80 people that night. I really enjoyed the evening and people were pleased with what I was able to give them. A second date was arranged for a couple of months later.

When we did the second demonstration, one of the local ladies came up to us and said that our previous one had caused a lot of fuss within the church community. They felt the work I was doing was devil worship. I do come up against religion from time to time, but I believe that we all have a choice and should be allowed to make up our minds we are all individuals and should not to be told which is right and which is wrong. I do not bring the religious side into my work, although I do believe there is something, I like to call it Divine Spirit. Spiritualism is a way of life, but could be classed as a "religion", in fact there has been much in the press about it not being accepted. I believe I am here to do a job for spirit and that is to communicate with people to show them there is something more that the physical life.

On this particular evening, the church had other ideas. They were holding an emergency meeting to pray for my soul! I felt quite honoured; no one has ever done that before. I didn't realise I was so important to these people and I am sure the prayers helped the energy in the room and we had lots of lovely spirit messages.

This was the second time I had connected with religion. The first time was when I was invited to appear on a local radio station. Roy Waller was a really lovely presenter and covered many subjects on his show. I had been asked to give a talk about my work and the help I gave to people.

When I arrived, I was told that to balance out the show, a Catholic Priest had also been invited to give his side of it. My own Grandmother was brought up in a Catholic Convent, so this wasn't a problem to me. I respect everyone's spiritual pathway.

Although the Priest was able to give his opinion on talking to spirit, he clearly did not understand or want to understand what it was about. He felt that meddling with people that had passed could not be right. Indeed there are references in the Bible that this could be done. He said to me "if people from spirit could communicate with us, why have I not received messages from my deceased parents?" My reply was polite and respectful as I chose these careful words "Have you ever been to see a Medium?" the answer was "no". I continued "I feel that if you had gone to the right person, your parents would have given you the proof you needed". I knew that his religious views would have been a conflict, but I felt quite sad that he would really have liked some proof from his parents.

We discussed all aspects of spirit on the hour long show, but each time I gave information on how I helped people, the Priest agreed that was his role too. So in our own way, we were both helping people in a different way.

As we left the studio, the Priest turned to me and said "I am not saying I believe what you do is right, but I do believe that you help many people". I was really pleased that he was honest with me, but it was a real shame he didn't speak those words whilst we were on air!

A Friendship Ends

At my home I arranged different types of workshops. When I was at Stanstead, Tony Stockwell taught us how to work in trance. When you work in a state of trance, you are allowing yourself to go into a deep meditation. In this meditative state you can channel spirit guides and other beings. Usually the messages are given about philosophy.

I had the chance to try out Trance and it was a lovely peaceful feeling. I have no idea what words of wisdom I channelled as I do not remember when I return back to my normal waking state.

I was working with a lovely man called Davey who was from Scotland. I gave him some words of wisdom which he said were very helpful and appropriate. After I had finished, Tony asked the group what they experienced. Sometimes the person channelling has subtle changes to the face, which is called transfiguration, which means they are overshadowed by the person working through them. Tony asked Dave if he had noticed any changes. Davey replied "Yes Sally's face changed and she became really beautiful" everyone laughed at this statement. So now I know if I want to look beautiful I have to work in Trance! I think it would cause havoc on a night out and I wouldn't be able to remember a thing.

I had arranged for a lady to come and do a day of Trance to teach people how to work in this way. The workshop was a lovely day and I again had the opportunity of working in this deep state of meditation.

The following day I went into the garden and noticed the Tulips were out for the first time. They were really beautiful and I told John they were finally in bloom. He came to see them in their glory a few days later. The look on his face was a picture; he looked at me and said "I expected them to be red". The tulips were a beautiful deep purple. He bent down and carefully touched their petals. I remembered the night on the beach and the gentleness of the way he placed the yellow rose in the sea. This was one of the rare moments that I felt privileged to have such a deep and sensitive male friend. The men in my life had always been so hard and rough. I didn't know at the time that it would be the last time I saw John. He had helped to inspire me to release my traumatic past, for which I was eternally grateful.

A few days later we had a major argument over something silly, as people often do. Our lives took a completely different direction on separate pathways. I was so sad, he had provoked me by letting me down on an important evening and I had said something hurtful, my fiery Arian temper had got the better of me. So we walked away from each other. I didn't think I would ever see him again and it was like going through bereavement. I was so sad; I didn't stop crying for weeks afterwards. I have no idea what it did to John, or if indeed he felt the same sadness. I learned an important lesson; it was to think before I reacted. That said, he was quite horrible to me as well and his words were hard to hear. I think this was the worst day of my life and I have had some pretty horrendous ones.

I kept myself busy with my work and tried to accept that the connection I had with John was over. In my heart I felt that it wasn't, but I had to get on with things. Slowly I started to get my life back on track, spirit kept me so busy that I didn't have time to dwell. It is not a part of my life that I like to remember, but we have to accept that we do have ups and downs in our lives.

June 2008 was a particularly stressful time in my life with work, family life and accepting the end of a beautiful friendship. I had sent a thought out to the spirit world that I needed to have some professional photographs taken. When I checked out the prices, they were so expensive. A few days later I received a call from a photo agency offering me a day in London to have a makeover for a fiver! I knew the photographs would be expensive as I had checked out their website, but I thought if I could just pick one that would be enough to use on my posters. I travelled down with a friend who was also having the same deal.

The day was really inspiring, I had my hair and makeup done and a really lovely photographer took lots of shots. We were encouraged to take along a few different outfits including some nice lingerie as well.

I was really nervous when I came out of the changing room in my Basque and stockings, but the lady photographer was very good and said it would be nice to do something different. So although I felt very self-conscious I put on a brave smile as the photographer snapped away.

We were taken upstairs for refreshments whilst the photographs were being put onto disc. I looked through the brochure and nearly died, the photographs were £75 each. I thought I could probably afford to buy a couple of them, but when the discs were loaded onto the screen, there were over 40 to choose from. It was really hard to find just two that I really liked, the photos were amazing and I certainly didn't look 49, I couldn't believe it was me staring back from the TV screen. I tried to choose, but in the end it was impossible. I had already paid £100 in advance as we were told that we would have that doubled up on the day. I had recommended lots of other people to have the same day so I ended up getting a package worth £1200 for £300 in the end. I was given a disc, so I had the copyright to all of them. I knew that I probably wouldn't have another chance to do this. I thought about how I felt when I was a massive 19.1/2 stone and how I would never have had the confidence to have photographs taken, so I looked upon it as an achievement for the weight I shifted.

I still cannot get my head round how differently I look today, the weight loss made me look years younger than my age, and I can honestly say I was half the person I was.

The investment to myself has proved worthwhile, the photos have been used on business cards, posters and everything else that they could be put on. My favourite picture of all of them is the one that I use on my website and is also on the cover of this book. I hate to say it, but it is one taken from the lingerie shot, although I guess you cannot really tell.

I was still working hard and was working at Worsted Festival. My friend had gone to look round and I was sitting on my own. An elderly gentleman came and asked if he would sit down. I told him that was perfectly okay and he started to talk to me about my work, saying he didn't understand it. He said that he knew I was interested in Paganism and we had a chat about that. He suddenly looked at me and said "You know the man you haven't seen for a long time that you keep thinking about, you are meant to be with him. You have a spiritual connection with him that cannot be broken. You will see him again and when you do, his hair will be a different colour". I was gob smacked and looked up to ask him about it, but he was gone. It was almost as though he vanished into thin air. I looked out of the marquee, but he was not there. I have this feeling he was not of this world and he was really an Angel. He was so old, he could not have possibly have walked out of my sight so quickly. His message left me puzzled; it came out of the blue.

That particular day, I had been thinking about how much I missed the contact with John and I had asked for a sign that we would see each other again. I took this message to be a positive confirmation that one day he would return.

Synchronicity, Purple Tulips and My New Home

Although I was kept busy with my work, I still couldn't shake the sadness of falling out with my friend and I wanted to run away and forget about everything. I always knew the bungalow was just a place to start my new life after ending my relationship, but I never really felt at home. The rent was crippling me financially coupled with the fact that I was having problems with a very damp bedroom and bathroom that had taken months to sort out.

I started to look at properties, but every time I went to view, they had either gone or were totally unsuitable. I spent hours looking at other places to live, but eventually I started to give up and realised that it wasn't the right time.

On my days off, I used to head to Mundesley. After John had taken me there, it seemed like home and it was a place I could escape to. I had always wanted to live by the sea and run a guest house. I used to dream of it from early childhood.

Even though my connection with John was over, I still had visits from his Dad. I was sitting in the conservatory doing some work on my lap top when he told me to look on a well-known property site. I had checked the site out a few days before and there was nothing on there that was suitable. A lot of the trouble I had finding somewhere was because we had two small dogs and landlords don't like accepting pets.

John's Dad kept on at me, until I finally gave in and looked. As I checked through the list of properties a house leapt out at me. It was in Mundesley, my favourite place and it was affordable. So I took a drive out and went to see where it was and have a peek through the windows. It seemed perfect! I made arrangements to have a proper viewing and when I looked round I fell in love with it.

I was really concerned about having it as my credit history was so poor, but my Brother had offered to be my guarantor. This was quite synchronistic in itself as he had refused point blank to help me a few months previously.

I told the agents that I would definitely take it, but I explained the problem I had with the dogs. They said it would be okay and that the landlord would be fine. A few days later, I received a call from the agents saying that they wanted to tell me the history of the house as they felt it may be a problem for me once I found out. He explained that the lady who lived in the property had taken her own life and would I be okay with moving still? I hadn't told them about my work, just that I was a hypnotherapist, but I was still happy to move in.

My children were not happy at the thought of moving so far away from Norwich, one of my Son's couldn't drive but he managed to find a house to share with some of his work mates. So I didn't feel quite so bad uprooting my family.

I had only exchanged one email with John since our disagreement and that was over a technical problem with a computer programme he put on that crashed, but I was left with the dilemma of the Tulips he had given me to look after. I thought it was only right that I contacted him to ask if he wanted them back.

I composed an email to say that I was moving away, I told him that I wouldn't tell him where I was going, it was up to him to ask if he wanted to know. I told him if he wanted his tulips back, he would have to make arrangements to have them collected. I had deleted his email address and phone numbers, so I sent the message via his website. I didn't get a reply, so I thought he didn't want to know me anymore.

Two weeks later, I received a reply from John, he said that he was clearing out some blog from his site and found it accidently. He said "so you are moving? Why are you moving, where are you going? Of course I want to know where you are going, why wouldn't I? As for the tulips, you keep them; I want you to have them. But make sure you look after them because I will be keeping an eye on them".

I emailed back and told him that I was going to Mundesley and that I would let him have my address and number when it was sorted out. He replied he would pop round for coffee the next time he was in Mundesley. I was so pleased to hear from my friend and that he still wanted to see me.

I got the keys and started to move my things out into my new home. I had been given the keys on the 7th August but because of the journeys needed to bring everything over, my first night was to be Monday 10th August.

I was booked to do a demonstration in Cromer that night, but Tracy was really helpful and arranged to bring all the large things over in a van whilst I was working, so she organized everything for me.

Despite its history, the house did not have a negative energy in it, but I felt the lady around me. The other Mediums I was working with came over for tea. We could all sense the spirit of the lady around us, she seemed very lost and in limbo. This can happen when someone passes so traumatically, they don't go straight over to the other side, but we felt we could help her.

We drove to Cromer and got ready for the demonstration. There were four of us working that evening. I was my turn to work and I felt a lady around me. She gave me her name as Caren and told me that she had taken her own life recently. As I was giving the information out, three people from the audience connected with me. I was able to describe her and give details about her life. The ladies in the audience were not family members, as she came from away, but they had worked with her.

In the interval, one of the ladies I had given the message to came to talk to me. She told me that they were all colleagues and that Caren had moved up here to have a new start, but that her relationship had broken down, resulting in her taking her own life. The lady asked me if I used to own a shop, I told her that I did. Although I was familiar to her, she didn't recognise me because of the weight loss. She asked me where I was living and I told her I was now in Mundesley. She asked me where about and when I told her she turned white. She said the lady I had given her a message from used to live in the house I was now living in. I knew that I was given the house for a reason because everything had fallen into place so quickly. The ironical thing was that the demonstration had been booked months before I knew I was going to be living here. But synchronicity played its part and I was able to give a message from Caren who had lived here.

I understand that life does become difficult sometimes and unfortunately people do take their own lives, sometimes we question why. The people that are left behind are the ones that struggle, but I believe spirit becomes peaceful. I do not believe that suicides are banished to hell, there are so many different levels within the spirit world and they go back to be healed.

I know I have helped Caren to move on and find the peace she craved whilst she was here. I have such gratitude for this lady. Even though her life ended so abruptly in sad circumstance, I have been able to help so many people since I moved here. Her life was not in vain and in her way she has helped me to heal the parts of my life that needed healing. Caren had only lived here for a few weeks and it is ironical that when she was so unhappy here, I was also unhappy in my own life. But I have great respect for this lady, if her life had taken a different pathway, I would not have been brought to where I am now.

A few weeks after this, I threw a house warming party. I had broken a nail on gone into Cromer to see if I could find a beautician to sort it out. I went into the shop and a lady called Carol said she would be able to fit me in.

As I sat down to have my nails redone, I sensed Carol's Grandmother, who was spirit side, standing next to her. I don't believe in pushing my work on people, so I tentatively asked Carol if she was interested in the type of work I did. She told me that her Mum had gone for readings in the past, but she had never had one herself.

As she showed an interest, I was able to tell he about her Grandmother, I also gave her names that were connected to her family, which she said she would check up on. As I continued to give Carol an in depth reading she cried when I gave her so much information from her Grandmother. This was the start of a lovely friendship with Carol.

I settled into my new life in the beautiful village of Mundesley. I woke up early every morning and raced down to the beach for a walk. I used to walk for miles. The sunrise is absolutely fantastic and as far as I am concerned, no better place to be.

After the busy city life, where most people ignore you, it was so refreshing to have people talk to you and smile back.

My life had begun again, I had been surrounded by some negative people and I made a decision when I moved to walk away from them. It took a lot of courage for me to walk away from everyone to a place that I didn't know a soul. I kept in contact with a couple of really special friends.

Some of the pagan group still kept in contact, but I had given the running of the group over to Annie and only attended it occasionally. As my work became busier, I didn't have the time to continue teaching and my development group was taken over by another Medium. As I travelled to Norwich less and less, gradually I lost touch with the groups.

I am a firm believer that people are in your life for a reason, season or lifetime and as I began to write this book I started to receive texts and calls from people I hadn't heard from for a couple of years. Some of the people I have chosen not to reconnect with as I don't feel there is anything to connect us anymore.

As I was working all over Norfolk, Suffolk and Cambridgeshire, my traveling time went up. I have at least an hour's journey to get anywhere now.

Last year I clocked up over 20,000 so I began to restrict myself to doing only two Body, Mind and Spirit Fairs. The two readings that stand out for me were done at a two day event on two separate days. The first reading was a young lady called Claudia, she was really troubled as she sat down opposite me. I picked up that she was getting married the following year, but I knew she did not really want to go through with it. As I continued with her reading, I discovered that she was in love with her best friend Mike, a man she had known from school. I cannot tell people what to do with their lives, but I felt that I had to explain that by marrying the wrong person she would end up making three people miserable. Marriage to me is a very serious commitment and to make such a mistake would cause so many problems. Claudia told me she was afraid to tell her friend about her feelings for fear he would reject her, I felt that this was not the case and that he felt the same way about her. I always believe that honesty is the best policy, so I advised Claudia to speak her truth.

I had so many people to do readings for and after each person leaves, the link is usually broken and I do not remember anything about what I have said. The following day I was even busier, but a young man came and sat down in front of me. I picked up that he was struggling with his emotions and found that he was falling in love with someone, but that she was getting married the following year. He didn't want to mess up the friendship they had, so he refused to give her any idea of his feelings. He was clearly struggling because his friend had chosen to marry someone else and he knew that their friendship would be over when it happened as she was also moving away.

I said to him that he had to be honest about his feelings to his friend. Ironically the cards he picked were Trust, Meditation and New Beginnings, which were all signs of the trauma he found himself in.

The best guidance I could give him was to be truthful to his friend and to see what she said. I knew that everything would be okay if he could tell her honestly about how he felt. He went away and said he would try and gain enough courage to ask how she really felt.

Later that day I was standing outside having a break, I had already seen six people and needed some fresh air. As I stood outside, two people came towards me holding hands. They were really excited and happy. I recognised them as Claudia, the lady from the day before and Mike, the man I had seen earlier in the day.

They told me I had really helped them, neither of them knew the other was coming to the fair and they had quite clearly come on separate days. Slowly the penny dropped and I realised I had given guidance to two separate people about each other.

Mike called Claudia to tell her he really loved her and wanted to be with her. Claudia confessed that she felt the same way, but was worried about calling the wedding off.

They decided they couldn't bear to be apart and that although Claudia had the terrible job of calling off her wedding, she knew that Mike was the one.

A few months later I received an email from the happy couple saying that Claudia had told her fiancée that she couldn't marry him. Her fiancée said he had been getting cold feet about the wedding but didn't want to call it off as he didn't want to hurt Claudia.

I believe that spirit work in the most amazing ways. The synchronicity that led to all three people being happy makes me so proud to do this work.

I love a happy ending and Mike and Claudia are now married and expecting their first child. I didn't like to tell them that baby number two would arrive before the first one was a year and half old! Sometimes, it is best not to spoil the surprise!

Since I had moved my life was a lot more peaceful. I kept in contact with John through the occasional email, but he still hadn't showed up for coffee. I knew he came to Mundesley most weeks but still the barrier had not been lifted. I emailed him and asked him when he would be coming over. His reply was quite cutting as he told me "That's a need you have, not one that I have". I felt really hurt again and resigned myself to the fact that I wouldn't see him again. I was already in a relationship, but I knew in my heart it wasn't going anywhere.

I emailed John with a message from his Dad and he responded back by telling me I had got the wrong person, but he also told me he had received a job offer in Germany. I was devastated, the thought that he was leaving the Country kept going through my head. How would I cope if he went so far away?

I woke up a few days later and just felt that I needed to make one last attempt to renew the friendship. Sometimes the things we say and do are not very nice, but I believe it is important to forgive and forget I kept wondering what I could do to build the bridge once more.

I don't believe in telling lies but something kept prompting me to send a text to him saying "Hi, I'm working in your area this afternoon and I wondered if you were free for a coffee?" I busied myself doing some much needed housework and suddenly my phone bleeped. I had a message back saying "yes I will be home, but I have to get up at 4am for work". My heart leapt as I read the message. I responded asking if I could see him at about 6.30pm. John confirmed that it was okay and that he would see me later.

I looked at the clock and panicked it was over an hour's drive away and I needed to get myself sorted and it was already 3.30pm! I rushed around getting changed, doing my hair and makeup and wondering why I had a million butterflies doing somersaults in my stomach.

I started the journey and was feeling so sick with nerves, I hadn't seen my friend for five months and I was feeling terribly excited but dreadfully nervous. As I was driving I asked spirit for a sign that our friendship was going to be okay again. I looked at the clock and realised I was going to be really early, so I decided to take a detour to the local supermarket which was about four miles from his house.

I raced out of the car and left my glasses on, no one ever sees me wearing them, and bought some chewing gum. As I started to leave the shop to go back to the car I looked up and saw John coming towards me. I said "Hello" and he looked startled as though he didn't recognise me, so I took my glasses off and I had lost more weight since the last time I saw him. I don't know if that was what knocked him for six, after all he was probably not expecting to bump into me, nor I him. He finally said "Hello, are you alright?" I replied "Yes, I am now coming to see you". He replied "Yes I know, see you in a while".

I drove to his house and sat outside. It was so good to see him but I thought he had aged, put on weight and his hair had definitely changed colour, a lighter shade and was slightly grey. My gentleman who I met at the Festival was right.

I finally knocked on the door, there was no answer, I knocked again, still no answer, the third time I knocked, he let me in saying that I should have just walked straight in.

As John went to make the coffee I followed him into the kitchen, he couldn't wait to say these words "I'm not going to Germany, it just wouldn't work out". Secretly I was relieved. As we sat down he shook his head and said "I've been a complete idiot" I neither agreed nor disagreed, I did not understand what he was referring to.

We sat and talked for a couple of hours, neither of us referring to the falling out, which felt strange but I didn't want to bring it up. It was in the past and I had finally been reunited with the man who had given me so much help.

John asked me where in Mundesley I was living, the road I live on is very long and I told him it was near the shop. We discovered that the house I was living in was next door to where his Dad and Nan had lived many years before and John could remember visiting it. I told him that his Dad had prompted me to find my new home. It is as if he knew I would find out the connection to the house.

It was time to go and we gave each other a hug, it felt so good being reunited with my friend. As I left, I said to him "I hope it's not going to be another five months before I see you". He replied "No, after all you live in my home now". John had been born in the village of Mundesley and had left a many years earlier. But he always thought of it as his home and knew that one day he would return.

A couple of weeks after I saw John, I was prompted to go and have a reading with a man called Steven Treadaway. I had seen Steven years earlier at the Spiritual Church; he was a young and attractive man and had a gentle energy around him. I didn't get a message from him, but the people that did were amazed by his accuracy.

He worked with a lady who had lost her young son. Steven told her that her son had been close to her and that he had seen his Mum sniff his trainers! What an amazing piece of evidence. I told myself I would like to be as good as him one day. I had never met Steven since then, but kept hearing his name so I was compelled to book a reading with him.

When I sat down he said that I was also a Medium and had worked at the same Public House as him. Steven only knew my first name when I booked and did not have a clue that I was, so I was really impressed that he picked this up.

The reading Steven gave me changed my life. He picked up on a gentleman around me and that I was connected to his son. He told me we were soul mates and were meant to be together. He described the personality of the man's son which didn't seem to fit my current boyfriend. I said to Steven I didn't understand as the person I was with was not the person he was describing. He laughed and said "not the young man, I mean the older one who's been around you, you have been connected in past lives, but you had an argument and you didn't see him for months until a couple of weeks ago".

I was totally gobsmacked at what Steven said, I couldn't really believe the information he gave me, but he told me he was never wrong. He had described my friend perfectly even down to what he looked like.

I went home in a bit of a daze, if Steven was right, the person I had been seeing definitely wasn't the one, but I knew that anyway, Steven was right he was much younger than me and the age difference would always be a problem. The past life connection Steven told me about made sense, it confirmed why I had been so sad when I thought our friendship was over. But as for me being with John, that did not make sense at all, he never gave me any indication that he felt the same, even though he knew I loved him with all of my heart.

I don't know what happened but my relationship started to fall apart. My head was buzzing with everything I had been told by Steven, but I could not see how he could be right. So I put the reading to the back of my mind and got on with my life again.

New Connections

Although I was kept busy with ladies evenings, demonstrations and personal readings, I stared to work in a spiritual shop once a week. Every so often I will have a connection to people I meet. One of these ladies was called Ali. I had done a reading for her in the summer but she came in one day and I knew she had recently lost her Dad. I told her that her Dad was giving her yellow roses and she confirmed that it meant something to her. I felt a real connection with Ali and I knew it was not the last time I would see her.

Around the same time I did another reading for a lady I had met the previous August. Karen had returned because she was really struggling with a connection she had and I was able to put her on the right track. Karen had brought her friend Mandy along. Again I had the same feeling that there would be more connections with these ladies. As it turned out Karen has been one of the most supportive people to me and without her, I would not have coped with certain things that have happened in my life. Karen is a very wise, gentle person, who has an amazing personality. She is always bright and breezy and is forever saying to me "Sally Taylor, never forget how special you are".

My work with Tracy was coming to an end and I realised that I needed to arrange some demonstrations for myself. I wanted to play some nice spiritual music and my favourite song is called Earth Angel, by Llewellyn and Juliana. I decided to email them to ask for their permission to play it and they told me they were more than happy to do this.

A couple of days later Llewellyn contacted me to ask if I would do a phone reading. I arranged to call them and Llewellyn said they had the phone on loud speaker so their daughter Holly could listen in as well.

As I started to do the reading I told them I could see them moving. Llewellyn said this was a definite no as they had just finished work on their house after twenty years. I was politely insistent and told them that I could definitely see a house move. I was being shown a beautiful white cottage with a white picket fence around it. I also picked up that Holly was worried about her exams but that she would sail through them.

I said they also had links in America and they confirmed that their business was linked with it. I was able to give them a lot more personal information and they were happy with what I had given them. Llewellyn told me he had been looking on my websites and he had been reading all about me.

I thought I ought to do a bit of research myself and went on to the Paradise Music website. It wasn't until I had done this I realised how famous they were.

After the reading Llewellyn and Juliana sent me some cd's as a thank you for working with them.

A few months later I received an email from them with a picture of a beautiful cottage, with a white picket fence. They asked me if this was the vision I saw in my reading I confirmed this was indeed the place I was shown.

Llewellyn called me to say they had been on holiday and found the cottage, but that it needed a lot of renovation. Although they had fallen in love with it, they had no idea how they would be able to buy it because of the renovations needed. They couldn't keep both houses.

I assured him it would be okay and that the cottage would be theirs. I received a follow up call from Llewellyn telling me that a really bizarre thing had happened. He was out walking his dog and bumped into a neighbour who was renting a place in the village. They got talking and the neighbour asked if Llewellyn knew of any properties that were for sale in the village, as they wanted to settle there. Llewellyn told him that they wanted to sell their place and buy the cottage, but they couldn't move in because it needed a lot of work. The neighbour said he would be happy to buy their property and they would be able to rent it off him until their new home was ready. What a perfect solution to a dilemma that they had all been worrying about. As I am fond of saying, spirit work in the most amazing ways.

Llewellyn is also a very spiritual person; he picked up lots of things as we were talking. He suggested that I change my name from Sally to Sally-Ann as it sounded better. I told him I would do that. Later on he sent me an email to say that he had done the numerology on my new name and it was a much better vibrational energy.

I have spoken to Llewellyn several times; he is a very kind and sensitive person. He also told me that he could see my picture on the cover of a book.

Llewellyn writes the most beautiful spiritual music and Juliana has the most amazing voice. One of my other favourite songs is called The Ghost. I would certainly urge you to check out their music, it is so inspirational.

I have not met this lovely family yet, but I have been invited to see the new cottage when they move later this year. I think what has amazed me so much is that Llewellyn has always been willing to help me, even though he is so busy and has come up with lots of suggestions for me about my work and retreat idea. We always think of celebrities as being distant and unobtainable, but these lovely people are down to earth and very special.

Christmas was approaching quickly and I had not done anything to prepare, I had been working day and night. I was really looking forward to having some time off and celebrating my first Christmas at the seaside.

I got up Christmas morning and took my daughter to her Dad's. The boys were coming over for a late lunch so I took the opportunity of going for a walk on the beach. Although I still hadn't seen John, I text him to wish him a merry Christmas and gave him a message from his Dad as I could feel his Dad around me. He responded back to me which was lovely. Although it was Christmas Day, it was very sunny and I walked down on the beach. There were lots of people walking and it was lovely to wish everyone a Happy Christmas.

Village life was a much slower place all of the people were so friendly. I didn't realise that there were a lot of holidaymakers that visit Mundesley for Christmas. I got talking to a couple who told me they had always spent Christmas here. There are so many people that come to Mundesley for a holiday and end up coming back to live.

The New Year proved very eventful and busy despite the warnings from the government about recession. But I guess that people will always want guidance and to contact their loved ones. In January I met a lovely lady called Kay who came to me for guidance. Kay's life had been up and down and she needed some positive guidance. I knew Kay was very spiritual herself and I told her she needed to be sitting in a development group. I was not teaching at the time, but said I would let her know when I started again.

I always know when I am going to have a connection with someone and as I did Kay's reading, I felt that we would become friends.

Because of the negativity I had been surrounded by, I had cut myself off from everyone and even the few people that had stayed in my life I didn't speak to very often and when I did it was on the phone or texts. I began to feel really lonely and asked spirit to bring some positive spiritual people around me. By this time my relationship was well and truly over I began to learn what life was like when there was no one around. I have never felt so lonely or empty in my life. If it was not for the fact that spirit kept me so busy, I don't know how I would have got through this time.

I had kept in contact with Carol who I met in the beauty salon and she told me the shop was closing down and she would be working from North Walsham. I went to see Carol there and I was asked if I would like to go in and do readings. It was good to be working from the shop, to be surrounded by young people and I enjoyed the time I was there. The girls were fascinated by my work and it was great when they confirmed that what I had told them was happening.

On the 12th February, I did my first charity demonstration,. One of the local rugby clubs had said they wanted to raise some money and thought that an evening of Mediumship would give them the opportunity. There were one hundred people attending and the group was made up of mainly young people who had not seen a Medium work before. The thing I have noticed with the young ones is that they don't often have people in the spirit world, so sometimes it makes it difficult. On these occasions I usually pick up psychic messages instead.

I gave a message to one of the ladies who had helped arrange the evening. I gave her so much evidence that she burst into tears. At the end of the evening she came to speak to me and said "thank you for the message; I didn't believe in this before I came here I was telling everyone who bought tickets that it was a joke. It was just an excuse to have a drink"

I was totally shocked, I take my work very seriously, I couldn't believe that people had come along just for entertainment; No wonder most of the people attending were young girls. But I couldn't help but be touched by her honesty.

I am normally a placid person, especially when I am working for spirit. I had become rather cross at being made out to be an entertainer. I turned to her and said "you give people the impression you are really hard, but inside you are like cotton wool". Her nephew was standing next to us and said "yes you are right; you have just described my Aunty to a tee". We all laughed and I knew that this was another person who had been converted by spirit.

The next reading I did was for a lady called Chrissi. She was in dire need of some guidance. There was a lot going on in her personal and work life. She also had lost a cousin who she was very close to. I knew her work didn't leave her a lot of time, but I had a feeling we would become friends. I told her about my friend John and felt that the EFT could really help her. When I gave her John's card she explained that she remembered him as a young lad, and her best friend at school had been John's sister.

I soon became friends with Chrissi and we spent a lot of time together. We had both recognised each other, but couldn't remember where from, we discovered that we had both worked for the same company in the 1970's. This was yet another strange synchronistic event.

Although I had continued with my emails to John, we still had not seen each other since the previous October. He was busy with his work and put his spiritual work on hold. He finally came to see me at the beginning of March and said that he felt he needed to get back working with the EFT. He told me he had been writing a book. I must say at this point I told him a year earlier that he would write three books, at the time he looked at me as if I were mad, I cannot put his words down in print, but I felt very smug knowing it had come true.

There has always been a resistance to accepting the messages he has been given, he believes in free will and doesn't like to be told he will do anything. I always disagree with him as I feel that we use free will to control our pathways. I am a firm believer that when you trust spirit 100% then there is no need to question, you just trust and go with the flow. My dear Gemini friend always disagrees with this one, so we have agreed to disagree.

Nevertheless, I was pleased he was going to go forward on his pathway and I said I would help him any way that I could. I had several other friends that did different spiritual work so I asked John if he would be interested in doing a presentation about his work if I could get enough people. He agreed and we set the date for 8th May.

At the end of March I received an email from a lady called Debbie, I knew that she was stressed out and I offered to fit her in the next day. I told her that her Nan and Grandad were around her and that Nan had seen her cry and didn't like it. Debbie was fighting back the tears in front of me, she told me she was determined not to cry.

I also picked up that she had a connection to China. Debbie was planning to do the Great Wall of China Trek to raise money for Rheumatoid Arthritis; Debbie also has this debilitating condition. Debbie told me her GP had said she was not well enough to go. I told her she was going and she was really pleased about this information, but she still felt she would not be well enough to go. I told her to have faith; it was definitely going to happen.

I asked Debbie if she had any questions and she asked about her friend Debbie who had died of Cystic Fibrosis many years earlier, she told me that Debbie had never been back to give her a message. I said to her that she would show herself when Debbie was spiritually ready.

I knew Debbie was on a spiritual pathway herself and that she needed to sit in a group. Debbie looked quite surprised and I told her I would start teaching again soon.

I also told Debbie I was happy to do some demonstrations to help her raise money for her Trek. We arranged to do an evening in Mundesley and we have done several evenings since then. Debbie and I became good friends. Debbie did complete her China Trek in October and was looking for the next daredevil thing to do.

Although I wanted to do another development group again, it was much later that I went back into teaching and Debbie came to sit with me. One day she gave me the news that Debbie had come to her in a dream, just like I said she would. I have given Debbie lots of message since from her friend.

Sometimes I go and see clients if they are unable to get to me and I had a call from the lady I had seen in the spiritual shop in Cromer. I went to see Ali and did another reading for her; I was able to get messages from her parents. Ali's life had been quite difficult dealing with bereavement and other things, but I was able to give her the information she needed to make sense of a spiritual connection she had with her ex-boyfriend.

Ali is a lovely chatty lady who is a Reiki healer, but she also gets a lot of inspiration messages from spirit. When we had a chat after the reading, I discovered that Ali had learned Reiki in my shop years earlier. I asked her if she remembered John as he was in the same group, but she could not recall him.

Ali has become one of my good friends and she also sits in the development group with me. I think about all the people I would have met if only I had gone in to meet the Reiki group at the shop. But we were obviously destined to meet years later.

Around this time spirit brought me another person to connect to. Nicky has also been brought into my life as a friend. Nicky only lives a few doors down from me, but since her reading has proved to be a rock. Nicky also told me that she had moved in just before me and was actually meant to look at my house, but another lady got in first. Had Nicky been given this house, I wouldn't have been able to move here and meet all these lovely people. Nicky is also a spiritual person and a healer and she also sits in my group. She is the one who persuaded me to start writing this book.

I firmly believe that people are brought into your life when you need them and my next important connection came from an email I had received asking for a phone reading. Brent had found my website when he was living in America. The strange thing is, I hadn't put my details on the site he found me through.

When Brent returned to England, he wanted to talk to me. He lives up North so it was too far to drive. After a couple of months of missing each other I finally called him and did a reading.

I felt an instant connection to this man and soon we were emailing each other regularly. He was very supportive to me about things that were happening in my life and I felt I could really trust him. I found I could talk to him about anything. As he lived over 200 miles away I never dreamt that I would meet him.

Brent told me he was a Graphic Designer, which didn't really mean anything to me. I never realised how important this information was to be. He also told me that he had been given a reading whilst he was in America and the lady told him he would be meeting a blonde haired lady who lived on the North Norfolk Coast. She could see him driving around the coast with her. Obviously Brent didn't realise the importance of this message at the time.

A few days after I started talking to Brent, I saw my friend Steven again. He picked up on the connection of Brent and I straight away. He told me that I would meet him soon as he would be coming to Norfolk to see me. He described Brent as a very good looking man who was kind and considerate. I am always amazed the thing my friend picks up on from the spirit world!

The past couple of months had gone so quickly, I had arranged the evening at my house for John and the other people to come and talk about their work. I planned on having around twenty-five people attend. I really enjoyed cooking and I was doing a meal as well as the evening. Soon the numbers reached thirty-three and I found myself cooking lasagne for everyone.

It was a fantastic evening and we packed so much in. Mark talking about Feng Shui, John did a talk about his EFT and Sean told us all about Nutrition and the effect that poor diet has on our health.

Feng Shui is an ancient belief of changing the flow of energy coming into the home by making subtle changes repositioning furniture and placing objects in strategic places. You can change the luck of the household and increase health and wealth. I first met Mark when he came to me for a reading when I had my shop. He also did the Feng Shui in the home that I shared with my ex-partner. He told me that the room in which I was working was detrimental to my health. I told him I had already suffered with cancer and he told me that he had not liked to say that was what could happen. He asked me to place a wind chime in the window to restore the balance and prevent other illnesses. He picked up so many things and advised me to make subtle changes to the home; I must say things improved after the changes had been made.

Mark also came and did the Feng Shui on this house and told me the things that I needed to make to bring in wealth and a happy relationship. One of the changes was to have a water fountain in a particular spot to bring in work. Sometimes it gets turned off and the work does slow down, but as soon as I remember to turn it back on the work comes flooding in again.

I had known Sean for many years; he was also a former client. He works with Nutrition and supplements and shows people how to correct their diet to enhance their health.

John gave people a demonstration on how we could use EFT to clear beliefs and emotions that we hold on too. He also told us how we could clear fears and phobias by tapping. EFT works on the meridians and is like Acupuncture without the needles.

We finished the evening with a demonstration of Mediumship and I got to work with my friend Steven who I had looked up to for many years.

It was so good to be able to work with John, I tried to support him as much as I could by giving him the opportunity to meet new people and talk about his work. I was passionate about his work and did everything I could to promote it, EFT had helped me so much.

John looked really well that evening and he seemed very happy. He knew that I had made him his favourite lemon cake; it is the way that I try to show him how much I care. I can't do it too often because he moans about the calories. I know he eats the cake as quickly as he can, he told me once that he had eaten a slice for breakfast because it was easier than cooking toast!

Something rather magical happened that evening with John. He was talking to my friend Karen and I walked past him to put the dogs outside. As I went in front of him, he reached up and held my hand, it seemed so natural. He of course says that he cannot remember doing that, but there were plenty of people that noticed and commented on it. I know that when John is totally relaxed and not thinking, his reaction to me is so different. Sometimes he brings the barriers up, when he is in a more conscious state. But I will always remember that special touch.

Everyone enjoyed the evening and we managed to raise a lot of money for Debbie's trip to China. The evening was so successful that I arranged another one for the following month. All of the girls I had met and become friends with came along and they got to know one another.

After the evening, Steven told me that my life was going to change. He reaffirmed that I would meet my client Brent within the next few weeks. I know spirit give so many things, but I also know that the timing can sometimes be out. There is no time in the spirit world, but we have our linear time and get caught up on expectations of things happening when we want them to. Patience in the physical world is certainly a virtue and one that I as an Arian have found hard to learn.

The next story I am going to tell you is a classic example of how timing can be wrong in our world. My client was a very troubled lady; she had been told that her husband had been given six months to live. He had been diagnosed with cancer, but as I did her reading, I felt that he had a lot more time than that. I told her that miracles do happen, although it was hard to convince her I knew she was struggling. She needed £2,200 to buy a scooter for her husband, so that he could be more independent. I told her that she would get the money she needed. I also told her it would be a good idea for her husband to have some healing.

She contacted me later to say that had received a tax rebate for the exact amount of money they needed to be able to buy the scooter.

As I said before, miracles do happen. Her husband continued his life for another two years. I can never predict the outcome, nor do I know when people are going to die, some things we do not need to know. But I know if someone has extra time, I just cannot say how long.

I know it is hard to comprehend how we can get so much information, but I don't really think it matters how. The fact is we can access spirit to guide and help us.

My next journey took me to the home of my sister-in-law who had a few friends that wanted readings. Even though I know people really well, I am still able to get information that I don't know about them. This was certainly the case that evening. As I started to work with Lynette I linked in with a man who had died the week before. I was able to give his condition of passing and his name. I knew that he died quickly and suddenly. Lynette confirmed that the evidence was correct; it was someone that she knew very well. The funeral was taking place in the next few days; I was able to give her details about the flowers and arrangements. Lynette phoned me after the funeral to say that the information I gave her was correct. Sometimes we don't know what is going to happen, but spirit themselves are able to give us access to their world.

At the end of May I had to take a friend to see Steven. Sometimes it is good to get a second opinion from someone else. We had stopped to do some shopping on the way. A bit of retail therapy goes down a treat. It re-affirms how synchronicity works even when we are shopping. We walked into a department store and I felt John's Dad around me. The music was playing and suddenly the song "Rule the world" by Take That was playing. In one of my nostalgic words I had emailed the words of the song to John. Every time I hear it play, it always reminds me of him.

As we were looking around the shop I saw a beautiful picture with purple tulips on it. John's birthday was a few days later and I wondered if I should buy it for him. I couldn't make my mind up, so we left the store and went into the local market. As we walked past the flower stall I noticed some purple tulips. It was very rare to see this particular variety on sale which is called Queen of Night. I pointed them out to Chrissi; she did a double take and went white, she looked like she had seen a ghost. I asked her what was wrong and she said "you are never going to believe this, but above the tulips I saw a sign written in purple the words spelt out John's full name. I took this as confirmation that I needed to buy the picture for him. We did a quick detour and went back to the shop to buy it.

We continued our journey and after Steven had completed Chrissi's reading, he insisted on giving me a quick message. His message was slightly different this time. He normally says the same as he always picks up, that I would end up with the same person as he has told me before. Steven always gives me the same message that this is meant to be. I was expecting him to mention this again, but he talked about my connection with Brent again and how I would meet him really soon.

After we left, I said to Chrissi "I know Steven has insisted that I will meet Brent, but I really cannot see how it can happen, he lives to far away".

I didn't have to wait too long for this as I received an email from Brent a few days later saying he would like to come and meet me and have an EFT session with John.

The Meeting

I had arranged another spiritual evening in June, so I asked him if he would like to come along to it. Brent agreed and we sorted out that he would see John the following morning after the evening.

I was intrigued by what Steven said to me about what Brent looked like, he had told me that Brent had dark, curly hair, a slim frame and was very good looking. I asked Brent for a photograph as I wanted to know what he looked like, especially as I was going to meet him at the Hotel he was staying at.

I work in a different way to Steven and I can never understand how he can describe people so accurately.

Brent sent me a link to his website which had a picture of him on it. Steven had described him so accurately even down to his dark, curly hair. This was confirmation that Steven had given me accurate information, not that I would never disbelieve what he gives me.

When Brent arrived he left a message saying he was waiting at one of the local bars watching football. I had booked Brent into a hotel but he had wandered up to the local bar as they had a widescreen TV showing the world cup. Brent has a passion for football and manages his own local team.

As soon as Brent turned round and smiled at me, I felt an immediate connection to him. I was really attracted to his beautiful blue eyes and cheeky smile. We had a drink and chatted for a while, and then I had to go and prepare the evening meal for the other thirty-two guests.

Brent arranged to walk down to the house a bit later for the evening. When he arrived, he was taken aback by the amount of people attending. He had never been to anything like this before but he enjoyed it and spent a lot of time talking to my neighbour about football. I told Brent that I had booked the weekend off so that I could show him around the area.

I collected Brent the next morning to take him to John, but after a mix up about where his appointment was supposed to be, we arrived back at mine. I thought I was taking him over to John, but apparently the appointment was at mine! At least I had the opportunity to show Brent some of the area.

After his appointment, we went out for lunch and I showed Brent some of the beautiful North Norfolk Coast. He bought me dinner in the evening and we talked until the early hours of the morning. Brent was so easy to talk too; he made me feel totally at ease. I was a bit concerned about spending time with a man I had never met, but we had an instant attraction each other. By the end of the evening I felt like he had been in my life forever.

I arranged to collect him on the Sunday morning as I wanted to take him into Norwich and show him the Cathedral. It was really good having some time off and having someone who was good company. Brent took me to my favourite Spanish restaurant and we had a leisurely lunch.

Soon it was time for Brent to leave and he promised me he would come back to see me again. This started to make sense as Steven had told me that Brent would come back again and stay at my house. Although I trusted Steven, I couldn't quite believe that Brent would come back as it is nearly a six hour journey; I thought it even less likely that he would stay with me.

Steven was not only accurate about Brent's good looks; also that he was very kind and considerate and treated me like a princess. Something I was definitely not used to, the other men I had been connected to never treated me well and it felt strange in a nice way.

I had a hectic couple of weeks and one of my readings had been cancelled, so I decided to go and see Steven work at a local pub in Norwich. My friend Karen came along with me, as she liked watching Steven and we went into the bar after the first half. While I was waiting to be served the man next to me started talking. He was with another couple having a drink. The man started to take the mickey out of Steven and was trying to engage me in conversation. I was beginning to get fed up with his remarks, so I turned to him and said "you have chosen the wrong person to talk too, I do the same work as Steven and we both take our work very seriously".

As I was talking to the man, the lady turned to me and said her name was Tracey. I could tell that her husband had recently lost his Dad because I saw his Dad with him. I took my drink and went to sit with Karen. A few moments later Tracey came over and I mentioned to her that her husband was really struggling with bereavement. She confirmed that he was but told me he didn't believe in the afterlife. I said that I understood what she was saying.

Before the second half I went outside for a cigarette. Both Tracey and her husband came out. He told me he couldn't believe that I knew that his Dad had passed, but I swore on my life that Tracey hadn't told me. I gave him the month that his Dad had passed, the condition of his passing and the name he was called. Tracey's husband was still sceptical, but I gave him my card and told him that I would be happy to talk to him when he was ready.

Sometimes spirit just needs to get a message across and I knew that was the reason I had been drawn to go to see Steven working.

Tracey came for a reading the following week and I was able to give her more information about her Father-in-law. They later attended a demonstration and Tracey's husband was amazed at the messages I was giving people. They had come to the second evening I had done for the Rugby Club and the evening was very different to the last time I was there. The bar was kept closed during the demonstration and everyone really wanted messages.

I linked with a young girl and gave her the name of her Grandmother. I said to her "your Grandmother is showing me her beautiful hands" she giggled and said "that was the only part of herself she took any care over". I went on to describe her Gran in great detail; I was shown a vision of an elderly lady sitting in a very untidy house, surrounded by clutter. She was watching Coronation Street and smoking cigarettes and drinking a glass of sherry. Sometimes I get a bit nervous passing on such sensitive information in public, but I always have to deliver the messages I am given. Fortunately the young girl had a good sense of humour and told me that was exactly what her Gran would do.

Her gran started to show me two budgies and I asked her if it meant something. She burst out laughing again, her Gran was telling me to ask what happened to the blue one. She almost collapsed in fits of laughter as she told me that the dog had eaten it. As you can imagine the audience fell about laughing and I was struggling not to lose my connection to the spirit.

I always believe that laughter is a form of healing and even though losing people is a very serious thing, spirit can still come through with their personalities and make us smile. Sometimes it doesn't always make sense to me what I am being shown, but I know I have to give the information as it may mean the world to that person.

The next story proves that we don't always understand the messages, but they are given in different ways. I was working in a pub in the back of beyond in Cambridge. I made a link with a lady and knew that her Mother was around her. I gave her details of her Mum and that she had links to Germany. I told her that her Mum was showing me a bowl of peaches but she was also saying something about oranges. My lady started sobbing uncontrollably and I asked her if she wanted me to stop. She shook her head and I continued with the message. She told me the reason I was given the German connection was that her Mum was from Germany. Her Mum had problems with some of the English language and always called oranges "peaches" which caused a lot of confusion. She came to see me afterwards and thanked me for the message; she knew I really had her Mum because no one else knew about the peaches and oranges.

I try not to work at weekends, but I had been so busy that I was working both the Friday and Saturday night. I had been to Norwich and was on my way back home when my mobile phone rang. I pulled over to one side and it was my friend Brent, I was very surprised as it was really unusual for him to call on a Friday evening.

I asked him if he was okay, he sounded really stressed. He told me that he was supposed to be going to Amsterdam to watch the World Cup, but the person he was going with had let him down at the last minute. Everything had been booked and he was waiting for the ferry, but he didn't want to do the trip on his own.

Brent asked if he could come and see "you guys" as he put it. I told him that would be fine, but I had to work until 9.30pm that evening. He said it would take him that length of time to travel to me anyway. He asked me to find him somewhere to stay for a few nights and arranged to meet me at the local pub. I tried a couple of places but they were full, in the end I thought it was silly not letting Brent stay with me as I had plenty of room in my five bedroomed house..

After work, I went to the local pub and found him having a pint and chatting to some of the locals. He looked at me and smiled and I gave him a big hug. I remembered what Steven said about him coming back and staying with me.

I told Brent that he was welcome to stay with me and my daughter rather than go to the expense of staying in a hotel. He laughed and said the last time it had cost him a fortune and he only slept in the bed because he had been with me most of the time! I wouldn't normally offer my home to people I don't know very well, but my intuition told me that this time it was alright and I could trust this man. After our first meeting we had got on so well and I was rather pleased that I would be spending more time with this special man.

I was working the following evening, but Brent said he would go off and have a drink at what he deemed to be the local. Perfect!

Over the next few days I learnt so much about my friend that I had met after a series of synchronistic events brought us together. He told me about his work as a graphic designer and offered to design some posters and business cards for me. I remembered how a few months earlier I had asked spirit for someone to help me with this.

He spent a few hours coming up with some ideas and chose an image that I had taken at the photo shoot the previous year. By the time Brent finished, he had come up with an idea that looked so professional and made me look like a million dollars! He told me that he would be able to email me the posters though each time I had a new venue and was happy to do the work for me.

Brent's work is fascinating; he is a really good artist and does work all over the world from his laptop. He spent a lot of years living in America and does most of his work for the Americans, as well as having clients all over the world. Modern technology certainly opens many doors. Brent spends hours working on designs to get the right image for the companies he works for.

It was really good having some company and Brent also needed some chill out time as well as me. We both work incredibly hard at our jobs.

I wasn't very busy over the next few days, so I had the opportunity of showing him the beautiful beaches and countryside in North Norfolk.

We spent a lot of time walking on the beach and just having fun, something that had been missing in my life for a long while.

I think it is quite odd how someone comes into your life and you just trust them instantly. I know we have been connected in past lives, so maybe that is why we get on so well. My failing is that I trust people too easily and I usually end up getting hurt. But Brent was different; he has a great deal of respect for women and treats them very well.

I was really sad when Brent had to go back home, but he told me he would come back to visit again, he loved Mundesley. After a fantastic week, my life went back to feeling very empty again.

I really hoped that Brent meant what he said and that he would return as I really loved spending quality time with him.

I am surrounded by some lovely friends who are so supportive and we spend a lot of time together, but sometimes you just need to have male company around you to balance the energy. Every woman loves to be wined and dined, and my fantastic friend certainly knows how to do this.

Loneliness

After the spiritual evenings I put on, several people wanted to have sessions with John. I used to take clients over to him or they would arrange to meet him at client's homes. I really enjoyed sitting in on these sessions, to me it is a form of healing as normally something else shifts in me at the same time. I learned a lot about how John works and how our emotions can stop us from going forward in life.

Shortly after Brent went home, I became ill again and I asked John if he would help me with the EFT. We had been working with a lady who lived close by, so after the session John came back to mine to work with my problems.

As we started to do some tapping, I suddenly realised where the illness had come from once more. I said to John that I thought I knew why it had happened, he asked me why and I started to explain. A couple of years earlier, when I had been going through an emotional time, I told spirit that I didn't want to be here anymore. He asked me to explain what I meant; he thought I had meant I wanted to move away. John looked quite shocked as I told him that I told spirit I didn't want to be on the earth plane anymore! He asked me why I had felt like that and what had started this all off again. I replied "it was when Brent came to stay, when he went back home I realised I was so lonely". He looked surprised, although we are friends we never talk about personal experiences. I then went on to say "I am so fed up, I work really hard to help people and work for spirit, but they won't allow me the one thing that I want" he looked at me and I wanted to tell him that he was the one I wanted, but I knew there was no way it could happen, I knew he didn't feel the same way and he has told me often enough that he is not interested in me other than friendship. At that point I just burst into tears and continued "I have asked spirit to bring me someone to share my life with, I don't want to do this on my own anymore". He replied "what you need is a companion" and I said "I want someone to do things with and be happy".

He said to me "I know you are not going to like this, but I want you to tap on "even though I am angry with spirit". So I did as I was told, hoping I could clear these deep feelings of loneliness.

John had told me a long time ago that nothing could ever happen between us, he had asked me to choose if I wanted to be in his life as a friend, he hoped I would. I was told I had to make the decision, but I realised that if that was the only part I could have, I had to work through it and accept it. This is the most difficult connection I have ever had to learn to deal with.

John always says there are two things you cannot use EFT for, it doesn't stop you falling in love and it cannot make you fall out of love. Believe me he is right, I have spent many hours tapping on that one and trying to release the feelings that I had for him, but I have reached a greater understanding of where and why I have felt this special connection to him now.

I accept the part that John plays in my life as a friend and a colleague, but every time he left me I would never know when I was going to see him again. We go for weeks without contacting each other and each time he disappeared my heart would hurt.

I knew I had to do some work on this one and I decided to go and have some past life regression to see where these feelings came from. I felt that we had been connected in past lives. I don't know how he feels about it now, but there was a time when he didn't believe in it. I hope that by now he will have more understanding about our connection and why I get so sad when he disappears.

Through the regression I discovered that we had been connected in at least six of our past lives and there are probably many more. John said recently he had been told he had over 400, I know he is an old soul and so am I.

I have already described the flash back I had when we went to Mundesley beach, how I panicked when he bent down to put the rose in the sea and I saw him being carried out on the waves. There was also the French connection when we were youngsters and my father wouldn't let me see him anymore after we had tried to run away together.

In my regression I described a connection to Atlantis where we were a priest and priestess; it was a very similar story to the one I told you about earlier in the book. We left Atlantis and went to Egypt to start a new life after the energy of the Island changed and it sank. Soon after we reached Egypt John was killed, I was his wife and I ended up living my life without him. It is quite strange because Egypt is a place that both John and I wanted to visit, but never have.

The next life I described saw John as a soldier at Baconsthorpe Castle; we were both young and were to be married. A battle broke out and John was stabbed, he lay in my arms dying. I was left to be a lonely old woman and spent the rest of my days looking after other people's children.

In another of our past lives John went to war, he was only young and didn't return and I again spent a lifetime on my own.

A pattern had started to emerge and I realised that he had always left me on my own, it wasn't his fault but no wonder I struggled so much when he went out of my life. I had to do a lot of work to heal these issues and emotions that I had carried so long. Now I am used to the fact that he disappears without a trace and no contact, but he always comes back eventually. I also realised that my love for him was unconditional and I could never ask him for anything in return, which I never have.

I feel that we are both in our last lives and will reach a very old age, so I have dealt with the fears I have about him and I know we will always be in and out of each other's lives. But it can still be difficult at times when I have no contact with him. Being a bloke he probably doesn't even realise what he is doing, but I have grown to accept that aspect of him.

The sixth life that I want to share with you is very strange and it involves two of my good friends Ali and Debbie.

I took Ali into regression first and took her through a few life times, in the final one she described a circus scene, and she was swinging on the trapeze! She really loved swinging up high above the audience and described the animals and people. She described the ring master and his daughter. She told me the ring master was very grumpy but that his wife had died and he was very sad and it made him very cross with people. She suddenly shouted out "I know who the ring master is, it is John". I was really surprised as this.

A few weeks later, Debbie also had her regression, obviously I am bound by laws of confidentiality and had not spoken to Debbie about Ali, and in fact she was unaware that Ali had been to me!

Debbie started to describe herself being in a circus tent and was looking at a girl on the trapeze. She said she loved the circus but was unable to work the trapeze any more. At this point she started to cry and get really upset and she explained that her Dad was the ring master and he had stopped her from leaving the circus years early to be with the boy she loved, the boy had been sent away. She told me that her Mum had died and her Dad, who she said was John, had stopped her from going as he was lonely from losing his wife.

Debbie continued to sob really loudly and she suddenly shouted "you were my mum, you should have stopped him. I loved my boyfriend and you didn't support me, Dad said I was too young and you agreed with him. You died when you were 51 and I had to stay here with Dad on my own".

After I brought Debbie out of the regression, I asked her if she recall any more details. She explained that she had fallen in love with a young man in in the circus, she was working on the trapeze, the young man had to leave the circus and the ring master (John) had said she was too young to leave. I had not stood up for Debbie and she didn't meet anyone else. When I died she was left alone with her Dad for the rest of her days.

It is really amazing that we have all been reincarnated as a soul group all of the people in my life have had past life connections with one another. They say that groups of people do return together, but in different situations. A husband can be a brother or sister or friend in another reincarnation, we can play different parts in people lives next time round.

I would really lovely to regress John, to find out his side of the story, if he can recollect it. With the girl's permission, I told the story at our last psychic evening, but obviously didn't mention John's name, but I have a feeling he knew I was talking about him. It can be so difficult when people do not accept past lives and the connections we have, but I hope he understands why I had to mention this as it gives an understanding of the feeling I have and we have to acknowledge them, in order to heal ourselves.

If John has taught me a very important lesson, it is about unconditional love and what it truly is. When we say we love someone unconditionally, we very rarely mean it; we want to be with that person. So if we want or expect something in return it cannot be truly unconditional love. It is probably the hardest thing I have had to learn of all my lessons, but I have accepted the part we play in each other's lives. John understands that I accept him as the wonderful person he is and I ask for nothing back. Just because he doesn't feel the same way, doesn't mean I cannot have the deep love I feel for him. I have learned to let him come and go out of my life, which has been hard. Maybe one day he will accept the special spiritual connection we have and we will be at a level where we can talk about it openly instead of brushing it under the carpet and ignoring it.

My health continued to get worse, despite working with the EFT, John walked out of my life again in October and I didn't see him for another three months. I really could not understand why he went away again, I needed my friend. He always told me that he did not want see that I was ill and had to visualize me as whole and pure. It was another knock back, but I realised that if I wanted to remain on the earth plane, I had to do something about it myself, I could not look to him to help me this time.

I had always told John that I would never let him see me wither away and that was how I used the EFT to help myself and clear the emotions that were dragging me down. In December I was given the news that the results had come back clear again. It was a terrible few months of worry, but I kind of knew I wasn't going anywhere. I used to laugh and say they wouldn't want me back, because I would give them such a hard time when I got there! I emailed him telling him I was going to be okay and he said it was the best Christmas present he could ever have, knowing that I would be here for many years to come. He said I had proved to him that I could change anything with my positive attitude.

It is important to mention at this time that we really have to be careful what we wish for, my thoughts that I didn't want to be here anymore manifested in my physical body. I was lucky that I had such an understanding that with positivity I knew I could reverse anything. But I must confess I had my moments of being really down and out of control. Through my experiences I would urge you all to think very carefully about what you ask for, as sometimes the results can be slightly different to what we expect.

In October I met another client who came to me for some help. Mandy had changed her life and moved down to Norfolk from up

North to start a new life again, she had separated from her husband. It hadn't turned out in the way she expected so she came to me. She didn't know anyone other than the people she worked with and I told her when I returned from Spain, I would catch up with her.

A few months earlier I had been looking on the internet and had seen a Guest House that was for sale. I showed it to John and told him I thought it would make a fantastic Spiritual Retreat Centre. He agreed and I forgot all about it, my mind being taken up with my health and everything else that was going on.

In October, I went to Spain with Ali for a few days, when we returned she said to me "I think we need to go and have a look round the Guest House" I laughed and replied "that would be good, but I don't have the money to buy it".

Ali was insistent and we arranged an appointment to view it that afternoon. The place was lovely, it was in great need of refurbishment, but if I had the money, I knew I could turn it into something fantastic. Ali was convinced that spirit would bring me the money somehow.

The following weekend Mandy came back to see me with her brother Malcolm. He was a really nice man, so full of vibrant energy and I knew he was very spiritual. He asked if I could do him a quick reading and I said that I would. I told him that he was on a spiritual pathway and I knew that he had seen spirit from a very early age. I told him that he would open a Retreat Centre and would be able to help so many people along the way. Malcolm told me that he had been giving the idea some thought and wanted to help people with drug and alcohol problems. I knew that the Retreat would be able to offer much more and I had a feeling that I would also be working with him to help. Malcolm had a lot of experience in this field and he has an ability that most people don't have, which is the ability to listen!

Before Malcolm left he told me I was welcome to visit him at Pennymead anytime I wanted to. It was quite bizarre because Malcolm only lived about an hour's drive from my friend Brent. Ali had told me a few months previously that she saw me heading up North to work, but I couldn't understand how that could happen.

Pennymead and My Northern Friend

In December, I was going through a very emotional time, I felt so low and I asked Malcolm if I could go and visit him. He was delighted and I arranged to go up with Mandy, who was travelling back to visit her children.

I contacted Brent to see if we could meet up and we arranged to meet in Durham so we could spend some time together. I found a nice hotel to stay in and Brent agreed to meet me there on the Saturday afternoon. I was looking forward to seeing him again, we kept in touch with each other on the phone, Brent is not good at doing the email thing, but I know it is much better to speak to him. I know I can call him at any time for a chat, which is really nice to know that I have such a lovely friendship with him.

The day before I went to Pennymead, I had sunk into such a low depression and I had decided to see the doctor. As the doctor assessed me she told me that I was severely depressed and I needed to have some medication to rebalance the levels in my brain that had become depleted. I hated the thought of taking anti-depressants, but I knew that I had slipped into a deep depression that I had to get out of. So I reluctantly took the prescription she offered me. I got home and took the first tablet.

When I got up the next morning I felt really ill and felt sick. I went back to bed and my face started to swell up. I got up and phoned Malcolm and told him I didn't think I could make it. He said if I could get to Pennymead, he would look after me and I would feel better. I said I would try. I went back to bed and there was a knock on the door. A friend had come to see me. She took one look at me and told me I needed to get to the hospital. My breathing had become labored and my face and eyes had swollen so much. She drove me to the hospital and they said I was having an allergic reaction to the tablets. So I was given anti-histamine to try and bring my body back into balance. I was due to meet Mandy at 4pm to start our journey.

I still felt so ill and went back to bed again. I woke up at 2.00pm and decided to have a bath to try and make myself feel better. I called my friend Kay and she urged me to try and go away as she felt it would do me good to get away for a couple of days. I went back to bed and suddenly woke up at 3.00pm. I was due to meet Mandy half an hour later, so I struggled to get my things together and drove over to meet her. By the time we had got half an hour into our journey, I started to feel much better and was glad that I had gone. I hate letting people down and knew that Malcolm would be disappointed as he had been out and bought a new bed for me. I didn't want to let Brent down either, as we don't have much time to spend with each other.

Pennymead was an amazing place, it had so much potential and I felt like I had arrived home. Malcolm has a good flair for furniture and putting fabrics together. He also has the ability to manifest the things he needs from charity shops!

He took me into my bedroom and I looked at the bed, it had loads of really comfy cushions on it and looked so inviting. I very rarely sleep, but I must say it was the best night's sleep I had for years! We had been up talking far into the early hours and it was a lot later than I would normally get up, but I felt refreshed and so much better, even though my eyes were still a bit swollen. Mandy had already left and because we had a few days of heavy snow fall, Malcolm told me he would be happy to drive me to Durham and then collect me the following day.

We arrived in Durham and the hotel was up the top of a steep hill. Malcolm's Jag slowly slipped up the hill, but eventually we got to the top. Brent arrived a little bit later and he came in smiling and greeting me with a kiss. He told me he wanted to show me the beautiful city of Durham. He didn't want to risk taking the car down again as the snow was quite heavy, so he grabbed my arm and started the descent to the bottom. I don't have walking boots and I was slipping and sliding all over the place, but Brent held onto me tightly and fortunately I managed to stay upright. I always feel safe when I am with him.

It seemed incredible that we hadn't seen each other since the July, we just slipped back to where we had left off and the distance between us seemed days rather than months.

Durham is the most beautiful place and we walked miles, looking at all the buildings and the Cathedral. We talked about everything that we had been doing and discussing plans we both had for the future as well. We visited several bars and eventually ended up in a nice Tapas Bar, I was impressed that Brent had remembered the place we went to in Norwich and he knew how much I loved the food

.

We decided to get a taxi back to the hotel; I didn't think I would make it up the hill especially as I had been drinking quite a lot. It is very rare that I drink, I didn't realise quite how many vodkas I had got through, but fortunately it didn't have any effect on me. I choose not to drink anymore; I always say I can't mix spirits!

Brent had to leave early the next morning; his football team was playing a match, so we said our goodbyes and said we would see each other soon. I watched as he left and started to miss him, even though he had only been gone for a short while.

Malcolm was on his way back to pick me up, but there was a hold up as one of the roads had been closed. I sat waiting for him in the small reception area, the feelings of loneliness rearing their ugly head once more.

Malcolm finally arrived and I tried hard to fight back the tears as we returned to Pennymead. Mandy was coming back a little later in the day and Malcolm's daughter was preparing dinner for us all. Natalie was living with her Dad and he helped look after her two children. I was not used to having youngsters around me, but it made a refreshing change seeing Leo racing about the house.

I felt a really strong connection to Malcolm and we talked about everything and anything. I told him about the guest house I had looked round, and he told me he would come and see it next time he came to see his sister in Norfolk.

We made our journey home and I called Malcolm to say thank you for his hospitality He told me he was coming down to Norfolk just after Christmas and asked me to arrange another viewing so he could see the Guest House.

By this time Mandy had moved in with me on a temporary basis as she was trying to find somewhere else to live, so it was nice to return the hospitality to Malcolm.

Malcolm arrived and we looked at the place together. He had the same feeling that I did when I went round and we thought it would be a perfect place to run a Retreat from. We told the couple we were interested, but we would have to raise the deposit money, a mere £140,000.

After much discussion, we came up with some fundraising ideas and I started to see if I could make the dream into a reality. We hoped we would be able to find the money needed by the following September. Life took me on a different road and aside from working; I spent as much time as I could fund-raising, I knew Malcolm would help me as much as he could, so we came up with ideas.

In January, John suddenly appeared in my life again, it had been three months since we had done our last evening. We sat and talked and I told him about my plans for the Retreat. I told him that I was planning to go and see Brent the following weekend. He looked a bit surprised, but after all, we hadn't spoken for so long and we never know what is going on in each other's lives. John is a very private person and doesn't tell me anything, only what he chooses to tell me. We spoke about his latest book and the fact he wanted to move back to Mundesley, it was his home town, so I wasn't surprised. I really wanted to ask him why he had disappeared yet again, but I didn't have the courage.

As John left, he gave me a hug on the way out and I asked him why he had walked away again. He mumbled "I had to; everyone kept telling me I was the only one who could heal you and I had to step back. I got an email from someone and knew I had to answer it, but as I started to type a reply, something told me not to do it". By this time I had known about the email and what had been said, it was not nasty just merely asking him why he couldn't help me. The email wasn't horrible, just from a frustrated friend who couldn't understand why he didn't want to help. I replied "you should have told me what people were saying" he said "I couldn't, you wouldn't have wanted me around at that time and you were better off without me."

I didn't realise until much later what he really meant. I feel that he really didn't think I was going to be okay and decided to step back or run away, whichever way you care to look at it. Although it hurt like hell, I missed not having my friend there to talk to. But everything was okay in the end.

Brent had been very supportive over my illness and was so concerned about me. We spoke often and he really helped me. He said that he didn't want to hear I wasn't going to be around as he loved Mundesley and he wouldn't be able to visit if I was no longer here. I know how much Brent loves it here, it is like his second home and he always welcome to stay with me.

I think it is so strange how different people react to situations in their lives. I don't think we can keep on running away from our fears; we have to look at what causes the feeling and work through it. To me, lack of communication is responsible for friendships and relationships going wrong. The technical world we live in means that people no longer talk to each other it is all mobile phones, Facebook and emails. How sad it is that no one truly has time for one another. I know what is like to get lost on the computer when I am working and suddenly hours have gone by, how frightening!

Life is too short to waste and I believe we should spend as much time as we can with the people we love. Sadly, not many people feel the way that I do. Don't people realise that all they are doing is being selfish, time is the most important gift we have and it is so precious.

I always knew that John would come back when he was ready; the connection we have is too strong to keep us apart. But I realised that I couldn't go on like this anymore and something had to change. I knew that I had to be honest with him and tell him that he couldn't keep on doing this.

Friendship is so important to me and I believe that true friendship is talking about how you feel, supporting each other with your problems and sharing with each other. I have other male friends and we spend quality time together, going out for meals and walks, but unfortunately John and I have never got to this level. Perhaps it is because he doesn't understand that I would be happy with this and not want anything else from him. I think it is a male thing, but I truly believe that you can be good friends with the opposite sex and not want marriage! Besides, we both lead very busy lives at the moment and I appreciate he does not have the time to share with me on a deeper level.

I need to be well balanced and focused in my life and the fact that John is like a boomerang in my life is something that I have to work hard on. Past life connections can be quite difficult if there are unresolved issues, so I hope that in this life, we are able to understand and correct anything that has not yet been learned. This way we both become the best possible people we can be and it frees up negative energy to help others.

Because the weather had been so bad, the snow had cancelled a lot of my work so I headed back up North with Mandy, we had invited Brent to come and stay at Pennymead and it gave Malcolm and Mandy the chance to meet him.

We arrived about 8pm the Friday evening; Brent had got there earlier and was talking to Malcolm about doing a logo for Pennymead. I went in and he smiled that breath-taking way that he does. God knows why this man is still single! But I guess he has the same view as me, when the time is right the person will come from somewhere. I really love the time I spend with Brent, he is such a special person and I am so glad that spirit brought us together.

I am so lucky to have three lovely men in my life, but I long for the day when I have someone to share my life with me permanently. But I have been told that it will happen really soon. Sometimes you don't see what is right in front of you, so I kind of think that I now know who I want to be with, but timing is so important.

Brent loved Pennymead and we spent hours talking again, he had some work to do so he had to spend some of the time working, but we managed to have two nights together before he had to return home to his football team. The weekend went so quickly. I think it always does when you have the company of good friends.

Brent spent some time playing with Leo, Natalie had gone to Turkey and Malcolm had been looking after his grandchildren for her. I have never seen Brent around children, but he was certainly having a good time playing hide and seek with Leo. I think he enjoyed it as much as Leo.

Although Brent had to work for some of the weekend, we had a really lovely time catching up with each other and again it was as though we had never been apart. Brent worries me with the amount of hours he has to work, but being a Graphic Designer is a job that requires a lot of dedication and he spends hours designing the perfect logos for companies to show their image in the best way possible.

Brent said goodbye early on the Sunday morning, I told him I hoped he would come and visit me, but I knew it wouldn't be until after the football season had finished. The weather had been so bad that a lot of the games had been cancelled and all of the matches have to be played, which meant the season wouldn't finish until May. But I told him that I would hopefully come back to Pennymead before then.

I knew that Pennymead would be really busy with the Retreat weekends and I told Malcolm I was happy to help him as it would take ages for my own to open.

A Budgie Called Derek

I had my first demonstration of the year and I was working for two of my favourite people, Christine and Trevor. I had met them in my shop a few years ago. The put on evenings at Bracon Ash, near where they live and also they also run a Spiritual Church in Shipdham.

I must confess I don't like the formality of the churches, not that I have any objection to them; they are a wonderful place for people to go to. But I do not like doing the philosophy side of things, I am not very good at it and get very nervous. So I shy away from them, give me spirit anytime, but ask me to do anything else and I shake like a jelly on a plate. I can remember the first time I did a church meeting I forgot to say Amen after the opening prayer!

Christine and Trevor have always made me welcome and I do not have to do anything formal. I can even mess up the opening prayer. Once in a church I forgot to say Amen! We always have a lot of laughs and this night was no exception.

I went to a lovely lady in the audience and told her I had her Uncle Harry with me. She said "I don't know why he wants to talk to me" I told her he was saying sorry, she replied "so he should, he was really rude and kept showing us his Willy"! I really didn't know where to put my face but everyone started to laugh, including my lady. I gave her another name and she said "that's my other Uncle, I don't know what he wants and I don't want to talk to him either"!

My next link was for a lovely Gentleman. It is always nice to see men at my demonstrations, it is becoming more frequent now rather than a rarity that it was a few years ago.

I knew his Grandad wanted to give him a message and I gave him Grandad's name in confirmation. I told him that his Grandad was showing me a blue budgie. I also gave him the name of Derek. My Gentleman became very emotional and I asked him if it was okay to continue. He said he was alright and I continued with my messages for him. After the demonstration he came to tell me that his Grandad used to breed budgies, and that one of them was unable to fly, he gave it to his Grandson to look after and he called it Derek. The budgie used to sit in his hand, it could not do anything else, but he really loved Derek.

I never stop learning and I wanted to improve my Mediumship skills. I had arranged to do a workshop with Gordon Smith and was going with my lovely friends Kay, Ken and Malcolm.

We set off in the car early one Friday morning; we had to go to Eastbourne, so it was a fair journey. Ken was driving and Kay sat in the front with her husband, Malcolm and I sat in the back. Malcolm had stayed with me this time as his sister Mandy was living with me whilst she found somewhere else to live. Malcolm has just come back from Turkey and had Turkish Flu for a few days, but he started to improve as we set off. I am sure he was getting healing from the three of us.

The journey was going well and we made good time, right up until we hit London. One of the main roads that we needed to go on had been closed for road works, so we were forced to drive through the center of London. The traffic was at a standstill and we were told that someone had jumped off the bridge. A few minutes earlier, I had been given a woman's name. No one in the car knew who it was. I had also been given more information but none of my companions could take it. We wondered if the information was connected to the person who had jumped, but we couldn't find out any details of what had happened.

We arrived at Eastbourne with minutes to spare. The hotel was really luxurious and we were all looking forward to the weekend. Ken and Kay obviously shared a room and Malcolm and I shared a twin room. It is so strange, I felt very comfortable sharing with Malcolm, and we had become firm friends, so it really didn't make any difference. One thing I have learned is that when you share with someone for the first time you should discuss what should happen if you have to share a bathroom. The first morning I got up early and Malcolm was peacefully sleeping, so I thought I would jump in the shower. I am only in there for a few minutes, but I heard Malcolm's alarm go off and didn't think anything of it. As I came out of the bathroom, Malcolm went racing in. Apparently he had been desperate, but didn't like to come in whilst I was in the shower. I laughed and told him it wouldn't have been a problem, after all we all have a body. Next time I have to share with someone, I will make it clear that I have no problems in that direction.

Ken and Malcolm had been put in the same group, which they were really pleased about. Kay and I were also put together, which we thought was really strange as we were at different levels. Kay said to me she didn't think we should be in the same one, but I said I wasn't worried about it and certainly didn't feel like changing after we had been allocated places.

After dinner we went to see the Tutors give their demonstrations. Gordon Smith was absolutely fantastic. Gordon is a very humble man and has written many books, which I thoroughly recommend.

After the show, we all went up to our rooms to rest up for the following day. The course was not structured in the same way as the ones at Stanstead. I really did not hit it off with my Tutor, which really didn't help. I got the impression from him that he thought I was a bit of a know it all, but when he saw me working I think he changed his mind. I don't feel we ever stop learning, although I didn't really learn as much as I had hoped, the weekend for me was about meeting new people and having some chill out time.

Kay and I both agreed we were there to help Ken and Malcolm who thoroughly enjoyed their class and the things they learned, they both felt more confident with their abilities.

I don't think I will be doing anymore courses, but the weekend gave me lots of ideas for when I run my own workshops to teach Mediumship.

John and I decided to put on another evening to raise funds for my Retreat, but this time I managed to keep the numbers to twenty-five. I love hearing John talk about his work, each time we learn a little bit more, and he makes everything so interesting. There is so much to discover about our fears and phobias and how to clear them. He has written a book about them, which will be available soon.

I decided to make the evening different this time I would do a talk about past life regression and how it can be used to help us heal from things that are blocking our pathways. We do bring fears and emotional things into each lifetime. If we don't learn the lessons given to us, we have to keep on repeating them until we do.

This time Malcolm came along and he brought dinner with him. I enjoy cooking so it seemed rather odd that I wasn't cooking very much. Malcolm does a mean chilli, but I also did a Beef in Ale Casserole, for the people who didn't like chilli. The meals are an important part of the evening, good home cooked food always goes down a treat.

My friend Paula came over and was going to do some Mediumship with me. Paula is great at Tarot reading, but it is only the last couple of years that she has been working with spirit. It was nice to have someone else to work with. That night spirit had other plans and Paula did all the messages.

I was unable to do the Mediumship because my Guides wanted me to work in Trance instead. I have never done this in public before and a few people were very surprised to see me doing this. When I work, I channel an angel called Josephine, she gives very inspirational messages and also talks a lot about the energy of the world.

This is an entirely different way of working and requires me to go into deep meditation. Only a couple of people at the evening had seen me work in this way before and the others were fascinated by the information given. One of my other spirit people is a young boy called Johnny who died in the war. He always makes people laugh and is very careful not to get told off by Josephine.

I always feel like I have missed a part of my life as I don't recollect anything that I say whilst in this state. There are many good Trance Mediums channelling today and both books and cd's are available. Ester and Jerry Hicks work with entities known as Abraham and another American Medium called April Crawford channels Veronica.

I am truly grateful for the life I have and I enjoy helping people. It is nice to be able to give people hope and show them how to trust spirit.

My life as a Medium can be all consuming if I let it, but I have many supportive friends to have fun with. Aside from John, Ali has also written a book of poems called Poetry by Alison White.

Malcolm is also writing his as this is being published. It is called 27p and Trust. I am really looking forward to reading it when it is published.

As spiritual people we are here to help and guide everyone who comes into our lives. We have a responsibility, both to spirit and the people we work with. It is not a pathway that should be taken lightly or controlled. When we are working with our guides and the spirit world we are following our true destiny.

I wrote this book after much encouragement from my friends. My dear friend Brent designed the cover for me after I told him about the story of the yellow rose. I think his idea of the rose in the sea was amazing, but he is the most amazing Graphic Designer anyway.

I wanted to tell my story to show everyone how our lives are full of synchronistic events and spiritual signs and how these events lead us to where we are meant to be and connect us to the others that we share our pathways with. Spirit have brought the people into my life that now surround me and support me and my work, without this help I would not be who I am today.

I really would not change anything in my past that has given me the fortitude to go on with life. I have learned patience, trust, forgiveness, loneliness, compassion, empathy and unconditional love.

The things that I have experienced have given me the strength to pass on my knowledge to others and also to empathize with people that come to me struggling with the issues I have experienced.

I bear no malice to the people that have tried to break me, they have made me strong. My ex-partner who put me through a living hell has taught me to forgive, without him I would not have had the gift of a beautiful daughter.

The spiritual pathway is not an easy one; it is made up of harsh lessons that we have to learn to understand. With this knowledge we become better people to enable us to help the ones that spirit bring to us.

I thank God every day for being alive, for the people in my life and for the thousands of people in the spirit world who have trusted me with their messages that have been delivered with compassion and sometimes laughter.

There have been many ups and downs on my journey but I am very grateful to spirit for bringing me the amazing connection to my friend who lives so far away. We may be separated by many miles, but my friendship with Brent is one that I truly treasure and I hope continues eternally. Sometimes we go for months without seeing each other, but as soon as we do it is as though we have never been apart. But recently we have spent a lot more time with each other, thanks to my Northern friend!

Brent does 16 hour days with his own work, so he has little time to socialize, but it is good to know that we get on so well and make time to have fun together. But Brent usually has to devote some of his time to work when we do, but I can live with that. I love watching him working on intricate designs, I never realised how painstaking it is to design a tiny logo. Brent spends hours working on just one design to get it right. I know the book cover took him many hours to do and I really appreciate the time he spends working for me.

My other Northern connection with Malcolm has brought so much laughter into my life. We have shared much laughter and many tears through our journey and I enjoy visiting Pennymead. I am working with him running Spiritual Retreats at his own sanctuary. We both have much spiritual work to do.

I could not have written this book without the pain I have gone through. But I know I am much stronger and able to cope with anything life throws at me now.

The experiences I have gone through with my friend John have formed a major part of my life and I hope he can understand why I have mentioned both the good and bad times that we have been through together. Without him, there would not be a story to be told, I would still probably be stuck where I was a few years ago and would not have met the marvelous people that I call my friends.

The last person that was brought into my life is a man called Paul, he has proven to be really supportive. He sits in my development group and is the most amazing healer. He is very quiet and doesn't say a lot, but when he does, I always pay attention to what he tells me.

I don't know where my pathway will take me next, but I trust in spirit and they will always look after me, taking me to the people that I need to be connected too. But I know I have the most exciting journey of all ahead of me.....

Epilogue

My dream is to open a Spiritual Retreat on the North Norfolk coast for people to come and gain inner peace and understanding.

There will be a team of hand-picked Professionals offering all types of Therapies to promote inner healing and peace of mind.

The Retreat will also offer weekend workshops where people can come and learn how to develop their spiritual pathway and learn to work with Mediumship.

The original Guest House I had found has come to a standstill, we were hoping to rent the property until we had the deposit to buy it, but after months of discussion they have told us that they don't want to rent now. Although I felt this would be a good place, I now know the place it was situated in was not right and I believe that it has been stopped for a reason.

After the disappointment I was inspired to look again and the perfect place has been found which lends itself more to the atmosphere I wanted to create. Spirit has told me the money will come from a beneficiary to fund the place which is a mere £650,000!

All of the proceeds from the book will go towards this project and fundraising is still on-going.

I trust spirit implicitly to put me in the right place and I know the funds will come, I believe in miracles, don't you?

So we will see what happens next and I am sure there will be Another Story to Be Told!

Thank you for reading this book, I hope you have enjoyed it and understand that the synchronistic events that happen mean we will all get to the place we are meant to be in the end.

Useful Contacts

www.sallytaylor.biz   Sally-Ann's own website.

www.THIRTY5IVE.com   Graphic design at its best.

www.paradisemusic.co.uk   Music from heaven!

www.clairebunton.co.uk   Image consultancy.

www.thecyber-witchcircus.co.uk   Emporium of wonderment!